2013–2014

Student Guide to
First-Year Composition

San Francisco State University

Sugie Goen-Salter

Tara Lockhart

Sarah Fama

Andrea Schriner

As a textbook publisher, we are faced with enormous environmental issues due the large amount of paper contained in our print products. Since our inception in 2002, we have worked diligently to be as eco-friendly as possible.

Our "green" initiatives include:

Electronic Products
We deliver products in non-paper form whenever possible. This includes pdf downloadables, flash drives, & CD's.

Electronic Samples
We use a new electronic sampling system, called Xample. Instructor samples are sent via a personalized web page that links to pdf downloads.

FSC Certified Printers
All of our Printers are certified by the Forest Service Council which promotes environmentally and socially responsible management of the world's forests. This program allows consumer groups, individual consumers and businesses to work together hand in hand to promote responsible use of the world's forests as a renewable and sustainable resource.

Recycled Paper
Almost all of our products are printed on a minimum of 10-30% post consumer waste recycled paper.

Support of Green Causes
When we do print, we donate a portion of our revenue to Green causes. Listed below are a few of the organizations that have received donations from Fountainhead Press. We welcome your feedback and suggestions for contributions, as we are always searching for worthy initiatives.

      Rainforest 2 Reef
      Environmental Working Group

Cover and text design: Ellie Moore

Copyright © 2013

For information, please call or write:
      1-800-586-0330
      Fountainhead Press
      Southlake, TX 76092

Website: www.fountainheadpress.com
E-mail: customerservice@fountainheadpress.com

ISBN: 978-1-59871-652-8

Printed in the United States of America

Table of Contents

Introduction

Introduction to this Book

Welcome to San Francisco State University, and in particular to our First-Year Composition (FYC) program. On behalf of the English department faculty, and the FYC instructors, we wish you the very best as you begin your journey toward a college degree.

The purpose of this guide is to assist you on that journey. You'll find detailed information about the FYC Program. You will also find general information about the university's Written English Proficiency Requirement for graduation, campus policies and regulations, the resources available to you, and some suggestions to help you be successful in meeting these requirements. It is our hope that this guide will answer any questions you might have and your first-year composition instructor will likely refer to it often. While it is specifically intended for students enrolling in first-year composition courses, we think you'll find it valuable in many of your other courses as well. Below, we give you a quick overview of what you'll find in this guide.

It is our hope that this guide will answer any questions you might have and your first-year composition instructor will likely refer to it often.

■ *Chapters 1–3*

The first chapter will provide you with an introduction to our FYC courses, information about the goals of these courses, and some general approaches used in our classes to help you meet these goals. In Chapter 2, you will find important information about the course options for meeting the university's FYC requirement and how each option offers a unique set of benefits to students. Chapter 3 contains important information about how to determine which option is the best one for you and explains "Directed Self-Placement," the process many of you will go through to select and enroll in your FYC course.

■ *Chapters 4–6*

Because your success in FYC is of paramount importance to us, Chapter 4 will provide you with some useful tips and strategies that will hopefully make your FYC experience a beneficial and enjoyable one. To that same end, in Chapter 5 you'll find a more detailed explanation of how the FYC classes are structured to support your development as a reader and writer.

We know that many students also benefit from extra support beyond the classroom. Chapter 6 describes the FYC support services available to you, everything from instructor office hours to tutoring and advising. Taken together, Chapters

4, 5 and 6 will allow you to show up on the first day of your FYC class already knowing what you can expect from us, what will be expected from you, and the resources available to help you meet those expectations.

■ *Chapter 7*

SFSU is a large university, and oftentimes it can be a real challenge figuring out the various deadlines and requirements. Chapter 7 puts all of this information in one handy place so you'll know such important things as when you can add or drop a class or how many times you can be absent from your FYC class. It will also fill you in on some important regulations having to do with grading, academic honesty, and proper use of electronic devices such as cell phones. We also want to make sure you are aware of SFSU's policies safeguarding every student's right to be treated fairly and in a non discriminatory manner.

■ *Chapter 8*

Like most colleges and universities, SFSU relies on technology for everything from how you register for classes to how you receive and submit course work. It's also the main channel of communication between you and the university, you and your instructors, and you and your classmates. Chapter 8 will provide you with a good overview of the technologies used at SFSU and in FYC classes and help you get started using these technologies.

■ *Chapter 9*

While the primary focus of this guide is First-Year Composition, we include in Chapter 9 the path you will follow toward meeting the rest of the university's Written English Requirement once you have successfully completed FYC.

■ *Chapter 10*

In earlier chapters, you learned about the many support services available to you that are specifically aimed at helping you succeed in FYC. In Chapter 10, we offer you information about some general campus resources available to you throughout your time at SFSU.

As you can see, this guide is chock full of information. Take your time and go through it slowly. We hope you'll refer to it many times as you make your way through your first year with us, and beyond. Once again, we welcome you to San Francisco State University and to our FYC program.

Please note that it is a university requirement that you complete your FYC class in your first year at the university. This means you should enroll in one of our FYC courses during the Fall 2013 semester. We look forward to meeting and working with you.

Please note that it is a university requirement that you complete your FYC class in your first year at the university.

1

Introduction to First-Year Composition at San Francisco State University

Administration

Shared Learning Goals

Shared Course Expectations

Integrating Reading and Writing

Administration

Composition Office	FYC Coordinator	Director of the Writing Program
HUM 209	Dr. Tara Lockhart	Dr. Sugie Goen-Salter
(415) 338-2128	HUM 466	HUM 105
	(415) 338-1711	(415) 338-7454
	email: taralock@sfsu.edu	sgoen@sfsu.edu

Shared Learning Goals

At SFSU, we value the diversity of interests and approaches that our teachers take in designing their classes, a diversity matched by the variety of interests and goals of the students who take these classes.

Our FYC courses might, at first glance, seem very different from one another, and in some important ways (described in Chapter 2) they are different. At SFSU, we value the diversity of interests and approaches that our teachers take in designing their classes, a diversity matched by the variety of interests and goals of the students who take these classes.

We know this course diversity might also be confusing, at least at first. For example, one FYC class might require students to publish their own individual blog while another requires small groups to create a comic book or submit a letter to the editor of a local newspaper such as the *San Francisco Chronicle*. One class might provide students with a list of required readings, while another puts students in reading groups who decide for themselves what to read. One class might explore one particular theme in depth, while another class might investigate various topics.

But we want to assure you that these differences notwithstanding, all of our classes are united by a set of shared learning goals (sometimes referred to as "student learning outcomes") and shared course expectations. This means that whatever class you happen to enroll in, you will be provided with opportunities to meet these learning outcomes. The learning goals for FYC can be grouped into the following five categories: (1) Reading/writing goals; (2) Rhetorical knowledge goals; (3) Research knowledge goals; (4) Genre conventions goals; and (5) First-Year Experience goals. (The chart below lists all of the shared learning goals).

■ *Reading/Writing Goals*

Because the ability to read and write well is basic to your success in college and beyond, our FYC courses are designed to help you meet particular reading and writing goals. For example, upon completion of our courses, you will be able to read **actively** and **effectively** and use information acquired from readings critically in your own writing. You will also be able to use writing processes and strategies for **generating**, **revising**, **editing**, and **proofreading** your work in addition to **collaborating with others** during the writing process, developing ways to offer constructive criticism and accept the criticism of others. Finally, you'll be able to **reflect** on your reading and writing processes as an avenue to achieving greater control of these processes and increased effectiveness as a reader and writer.

To help you meet these goals, your instructor will provide you with a variety of opportunities to share your reading and writing with your classmates. In addition to receiving constructive feedback from your classmates on your drafts-in-progress and how to make productive use of that feedback, you will also gain skill in providing insightful feedback to your classmates. Since practicing reading other's work critically helps us become better readers of our own work, activities such as **peer review** have a double purpose: you offer constructive feedback to others but you also learn how to be a smarter writer and reviser in the process. You will also have numerous opportunities to think about (reflect on) what you are learning as a reader and writer.

■ *Rhetorical Knowledge Goals*

Rhetorical knowledge is the ability to act on your understanding of the situational influences that affect the choices a writer makes. These influences include who your audience is and what the purpose is for writing, as well as what form and medium (genre) the writing will take.

In order for you to develop this understanding, you can expect that your instructor will introduce you to a variety of reading and writing assignments that help you see how writing can be used for different purposes and/or to reach different audiences and can be made available using different media. In addition to written essays, FYC teachers typical provide students with opportunities to write other genres such as autobiographical narratives, journal entries, opinion pieces, critical reviews, and research reports, to name only a few. Many instructors also have their students read and write using different digital media such as blogs, wikis, podcasts, YouTube, websites, not to mention social networking sites like Facebook and Twitter.

■ *Genre Convention Goals*

Another important learning goal of our FYC courses is for you to develop knowledge of genre conventions—everything from how to arrange and structure your writing, to knowing how to organize your paragraphs to things like how your writing "sounds" (what we refer to as "tone" or "voice"). We also want you to learn to proofread for grammar features, punctuation, and spelling so that your writing is well received and your meaning is clear.

■ *Research Knowledge Goals*

One of the most important and difficult challenges in all academic writing is the ability to put our ideas side by side the ideas of others, to join our thinking with others who have thought about that same topic. In our FYC courses, you will gain important practice in locating the ideas of others and then using them in your own writing in thoughtful ways, and in ways that give appropriate credit to the ideas of others. Specifically, you will learn to create and apply a research plan to locate, use, and evaluate information from a variety of sources, including library resources. You will also practice using evidence and analysis to successfully support the central purpose of your writing and to demonstrate ethical conduct in your writing and the appropriate use and citation of the works of others.

In short, you will learn how to educate yourself about a topic, and then "join the conversation" by adding your perspective in academically appropriate ways.

■ *First-Year Experience Goals*

Finally, because you begin taking our FYC courses in your very first semester at the university, we think it's important that our courses provide you with opportunities to get comfortable and familiar with the campus, connect with the university, and start to think of San Francisco State as home. We want you to gain and use this knowledge of the university community to support your development as a learner, reader, and writer.

FYC Shared Learning Goals

Reading/Writing Goals	1. Students will read actively and effectively and use information acquired from readings, research, and other sources critically in their own writing.
	2. Students will use writing processes and strategies for generating, revising, editing, and proofreading their work; collaborate with others during the writing process, developing ways to offer constructive criticism and accept the criticism of others.
	3. Students will reflect on their reading and writing processes as an avenue to achieving greater control of these processes and increased effectiveness as readers and writers.
Rhetorical Knowledge Goals	4. Students will demonstrate a basic familiarity with rhetorical conventions, composing effective expository prose with regard to purpose, audience, and genre.
Genre Knowledge Goals	5. Students will develop knowledge of genre conventions ranging from structure and paragraphing to tone and mechanics; control such surface features as syntax, grammar, punctuation, and spelling.
Research Knowledge Goals	6. Students will create and apply a research plan to locate, use, and evaluate information from a variety of sources, including library resources.
	7. Students will use evidence and analysis to successfully support the central purpose of their writing; demonstrate ethical conduct in their writing and the appropriate use and citation of the works of others.
First-Year Experience Goals	8. Students will gain and use knowledge of the academic community to support their development as learners, readers, and writers.

Shared Course Expectations

In addition to shared learning goals, the FYC courses are also united by shared course expectations. What this means is that no matter what FYC class you enroll in, you can expect that all of our FYC classes will meet the following requirements.

Shared Course Expectations	
University Expectations	1. All of our FYC courses are lower division. The units count toward graduation and satisfy the university's first-year written composition requirement.
	2. The grading in your course will be ABC/NC.
	3. You will write 6,000–7,000 words with an opportunity for practice and feedback; revisions are included in the number of words.
Reading/ Writing Expectations	4. The readings in your FYC class will be drawn from a variety of sources, representing the perspectives from a range of academic majors and intellectual traditions.
	5. The readings and writing assignments in your class will ask you to be self-reflective, to think about yourself as a student, learner, and citizen of this world, both locally and globally. In short, you will be asked to think about the reading and writing you do in this course for what it means for you personally and in the world you inhabit.
	6. At least one of the assignments in your course will address some aspect of being a college student. You might be asked to write a personal history of yourself as a student; you might be asked to write a review of a campus artistic event or lecture you attend; you might be assigned to explore a field of study and its related career opportunities or do a research-based analysis of issues facing new college students.
	7. At least one assignment will be to write an argumentative or persuasive essay on a particular topic that your class is exploring.
	8. At least one of your assignments will involve doing research: finding sources, including using the library, and using these sources effectively and ethically in your writing.
Portfolio Expectations	9. All FYC courses will require students to submit their work in a final portfolio. Your portfolio will consist of a reflective cover letter that introduces the portfolio to your instructor. With your instructor's guidance, you will select three written assignments to include, at least one of which will be an analytic or persuasive essay and one of which will be based on research.

Integrating Reading and Writing

This is an exciting time for you as you enter college and begin your journey toward a college degree and the rewards that a college degree can offer. It's also an exciting time because you get to participate in an approach to meeting SFSU's first-year composition requirement that takes advantage of the important connection between reading and writing.

For some time, educators have known that there is a relationship between learning to read and learning to write. For example, we know that students who are successful at college-level writing also happen to be successful readers. We also know that less experienced readers tend to not do very well at college-level writing tasks. We know, too, that when students improve in their reading, they will see improvements in their writing, and vice versa.

. . . when students improve in their reading, they will see improvements in their writing, and vice-versa.

SFSU's FYC program puts all that we know about the relationship of reading and writing into practice. Since virtually all learning, regardless of academic interests and personal and professional goals, involves being able to read and write effectively, you are fortunate to get to participate in a program where you get to experience this reading/writing relationship, to read about what you write, to apply skills you learn in reading to further develop your skills as a writer, and to apply skills you learn in writing to develop as a reader.

In short, the purpose of the FYC program is to help you develop further as a reader and writer and, as a result, to become a more reflective and critical thinker. We expect you to leave our program able to effectively manage the many reading and writing situations that you will experience at SFSU and beyond. To meet these goals, you will have to do a lot of work, but if you work hard and complete all of the assignments to the best of your ability, we are sure that your success and confidence as a learner will grow.

Our FYC courses are designed so that you can experience how every act of writing involves reading, and how every act of reading involves writing . . .

Our FYC courses are designed so that you can experience how *every* act of writing involves reading, and how *every* act of reading involves writing; therefore, as your writing develops, so too will your reading proficiency, and vice versa. To make sure you experience this connection, your teacher will provide you with assignments that do the following:

- **Start with what you already know.** Each of you brings to this classroom your own life experience, wisdom, and insights. This is called your *schema* (pronounced *"skeema")*. It's the information and the structures your brain already holds before you even walk into this classroom. And this schema will be the foundation upon which you and your instructor build.

- **Use writing to read.** You can expect that your instructor will have you "annotate" texts, for example, making notes while you read, keeping a reading journal, etc. In this way, you will use writing to help you reach deeper understanding of what you read.

- **Ask you to write about what you find difficult in reading.** All of us experience difficulty when we read, places in the text where we encounter words or ideas that we find hard to understand. These are places where real learning can occur, so your instructor will provide you with activities and assignments that ask you to use writing to work through these important difficulties.

- **Use reading to write.** You can expect that your instructor will ask you to look at what you read, not only for what is says, but for *how* it says it. By looking at what the writer did, the choices he or she made, you learn valuable tools for how to put together your own pieces of writing. We call this reading "rhetorically."

- **Ask you to "mine the text" for grammatical features.** This means when you read something, your instructor will ask you to notice how the writer put together his or her sentences, how he or she introduced a quote, for example, or joined ideas together. In this way you will learn how to develop your sentences grammatically by using the example of the writers you read.

- **Ask you to be self-reflective.** This means that your instructor will ask you to think and write about your experiences with reading and writing, in particular, what reading taught you about how to write and what writing teaches you about reading. In this way, you will be sure to experience how reading and writing are interconnected and how this connection helps promote critical thinking. Being reflective will also help you to see how you can use what you learn in FYC in other courses and perhaps even your life outside of school.

2

The FYC Courses

English 114

Stretch English 104/105

Composition for Multilingual Students (CMS)

SFSU offers three different options for meeting the First-Year Composition Requirement:

1. The Semester-long Program (English 114)

2. The Year-long Program (Stretch English 104/105)

3. The Composition for Multilingual Students (CMS) Program

English 114

English 114 is a 3-credit, single semester version of FYC. Once students successfully complete ENG 114, they have completed SFSU's First-Year Written Composition requirement and have earned 3 credits toward the 120 needed for graduation.

Because students complete English 114 in a single semester, the pace is quicker than in Stretch English 104/105. The class size in English 114 is also slightly larger (20 students compared to 18 in the stretch course).

English 114 is a good option if you feel confident about your ability to meet the FYC learning goals and course expectations listed in Chapter 1, and don't feel the extra time offered by the year-long stretch course is necessary or beneficial for you. In our experience teaching these courses, we find that some students actually need the faster pace to feel challenged and motivated. Even so, if you enroll in ENG 114 and find you need some additional help, you still have access to the same wide variety of tutoring and other support services as students who enroll in the stretch course.

English 114 is a good option if you feel confident about your ability to meet the FYC learning goals and course expectations listed in Chapter 1 . . .

All of our FYC classes meet for 3 hours per week (At SFSU, an "hour" of class time is actually 50 minutes.) We offer English 114 classes throughout the week, in a variety of time slots. Some of our English 114 classes meet 3 times a week, Mondays, Wednesdays, and Fridays for 50 minutes each class session. Some of our English 114 classes meet twice a week (Monday/Wednesday or Tuedsay/Thursday) for 75 minutes each. We also have some evening English 114 classes that meet once a week for three hours (with a ten-minute break).

Stretch English 104/105

Stretch English 104/105 is SFSU's year-long version of First-Year Composition. We call it the "stretch" program because we stretch course expectations and learning goals over a full year rather than a single semester. Students who complete the stretch course earn 6 units of credit (3 units each semester), all of which count toward the 120 units needed to graduate. Once students successfully complete

English 104/105, they have met the university's First-Year Composition requirement.

Stretch FYC classes meet twice a week, for 75 minutes each session. Some classes meet Mondays and Wednesdays and others meet on Tuesdays and Thursdays. We offer these classes at a variety of times throughout the day, beginning at 8:10 in the morning.

As you learned in Chapter 1, English 104/105 shares the same student learning goals and course expectations as English 114 and our Composition for Multilingual Students (CMS) courses. Students who choose this stretch option enroll in English 104 in fall and English 105 in spring during their first year at SFSU. Since English 104/105 is one year-long course, students will have the same instructor and group of classmates in the spring semester as they had in the fall semester. The class will also meet at the same day and time during both semesters. This will help when it comes time to plan the rest of your class schedule.

English 104/105 is a single class stretched over two semesters. Even so, the University requires your instructor to assign you a grade at the end of the English 104 half of the class. But because the class is only halfway through, the grade you receive in English 104 should be seen as a mid-course progress report, an indicator of where you stand as you go into the second half of the class.

Please note that if a student quits attending class regularly and/or turning in the assigned work during the English 104 semester, the instructor will assign a "No Credit" grade (NC) at the end of English 104, which prohibits the student from being allowed to continue with the class into the second, English 105, half of the course. It is the University's policy that students complete their FYC classes in their first year. Anyone who gets an NC in the English 104 half of the class and therefore can't go on to the second half of the class will face potentially serious consequences in terms of their continued enrollment at SFSU. Please, don't let this happen to you. We provide you with some good tips to help you avoid this in Chapter 4.

You might be wondering at this point why someone would choose to take a year-long class when they can complete the same requirement in a single semester. In our experience, the students who are well suited to the stretch option are those who think they'd benefit from some extra help afforded by more time and individual assistance. Remember, English 114 and Stretch English 104/105 all meet the same requirements listed in Chapter 1. Students in either option will compile a final portfolio; the stretch course just does it at a slower pace, allowing learning to happen more gradually. And since all 6 of the credits count toward graduation, there is no real advantage to taking FYC in a single semester if you think the extra time and assistance will increase your chances for success.

In our experience, the students who are well-suited to the stretch option are those who think they'd benefit from some extra help afforded by more time and individual assistance.

Composition for Multilingual Students (CMS)

The Composition for Multilingual Students program (CMS) is designed for students who are non native speakers of English. CMS courses fulfill the same university requirement for First-Year Composition as do our stretch course, English 104/105 and English 114. Our CMS courses are designed specifically to meet the learning needs of multilingual students, including speech and grammar instruction that is not available in either our stretch course, English 104/105, or in English 114. Even if you did not take ESL classes in high school and you speak English fluently, if English is not your first or primary language, our CMS courses may be appropriate for you. Completing your writing requirements in the CMS program will not delay your graduation since **all** of the units earned in CMS courses count toward the 120 units needed to graduate.

The charts below show the various pathways for successful completion of SFSU's First-Year Composition Requirement. Once students are able to "Go to ENG 214" (or "Go to ENG 310" for students in CMS), they have met the FYC requirement.

Whatever option you think is best for you, English 114, stretch English 104/105, or our CMS program, the next chapter will provide you with additional information to help you choose. Chapter 3 will also tell you what procedures you need to follow to help you make the best choice possible.

> *Even if you did not take ESL classes in high school and you speak English fluently, if English is not your first or primary language, our CMS courses may be appropriate for you.*

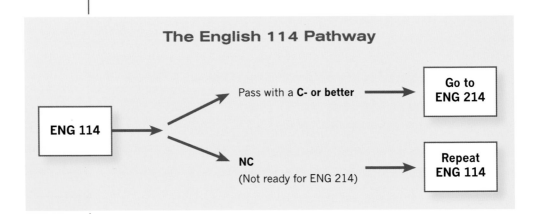

The English 114 Pathway

ENG 114 → Pass with a **C- or better** → **Go to ENG 214**

ENG 114 → NC (Not ready for ENG 214) → **Repeat ENG 114**

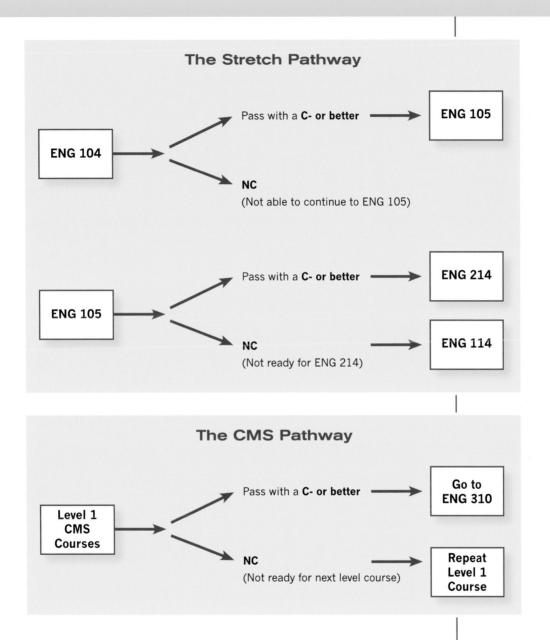

The Stretch Pathway

ENG 104 → Pass with a **C- or better** → **ENG 105**

NC
(Not able to continue to ENG 105)

ENG 105 → Pass with a **C- or better** → **ENG 214**

NC
(Not ready for ENG 214) → **ENG 114**

The CMS Pathway

Level 1 CMS Courses → Pass with a **C- or better** → **Go to ENG 310**

NC
(Not ready for next level course) → **Repeat Level 1 Course**

3

Choosing the
Best Course for You

Directed Self-Placement (DSP)

San Francisco State University has designed an online application for placing students in first-year composition classes. This application is called Directed Self-Placement (DSP). If your **EPT score is 138–146**, you are **required** to use this application to help you decide which of our three FYC options is best for you. There is no cost associated with DSP; it is free of charge.

> ### NOTE
>
> For students entering Fall 2013, if your EPT score is ABOVE 146, you do not need to DSP. You will enroll in English 114 during new student orientation. You also do not need to read Chapter 3; you can skip to Chapter 4.
>
> For students with EPT scores LOWER THAN 138, you will complete DSP as part of your Early Start English class. For more information about SFSU's Early Start Program, please go to http://www.sfsu.edu/~advising/esp/home.html.

We believe that, with good guidance from us, you are the best person to choose which first-year composition course is best for you. You know what your background and experiences with reading and writing have been. You also know how motivated and confident you are, what your goals are, and what support systems you have in place to help you meet those goals. You now have the opportunity to make an important decision about which composition class is best for you (that is the "self-placement" part of DSP). Our job is to provide you with some additional guidance to help you make the best choice possible (that is the "directed" part of DSP). As detailed in Chapter 2, you have three options to choose from:

1. The Semester-Long Program: English 114

2. The Year-Long Program: Stretch English 104/105

3. The Composition for Multilingual Students Program

DSP and the English 114 Choice

English 114 is a 3-credit, single semester version of FYC. Once students successfully complete ENG 114, they have completed SFSU's First-Year Written Composition requirement and have earned 3 credits toward the 120 needed for graduation. Because students complete English 114 in a single semester, the pace is quicker than in Stretch English 104/105. The class size in English 114 is also slightly larger (20 students compared to 18 in the stretch course).

*If your **EPT score is 138–146**, you are **required** to use this application to help you decide which of our three FYC options is best for you.*

■ *Why Choose English 114?*

There are at least three benefits to choosing English 114 compared to Stretch English 104/105:

1. English 114 is a good choice if you feel confident about your reading and writing abilities and don't feel the extra time offered by the year long stretch course is necessary or beneficial for you.

2. In our experience teaching these courses, we find that some students actually need a faster pace to feel challenged and motivated. Even so, if you find you need some additional help, you still have access to the same wide variety of tutoring and other support services as students who enroll in the stretch course.

3. Students earn 3 credits toward the 120 needed for graduation and can advance to the next level composition course (English 214) the following semester, thereby completing both the university's First and Second Year composition requirements in a single year.

DSP and the "Stretch" English 104/105 Choice

English 104/105 is SFSU's year long version of First-Year Composition. We call it the "stretch" program because we stretch course expectations and learning goals over a full year rather than a single semester. Students who complete the stretch course earn 6 units of credit (3 units each semester), all of which count toward the 120 units needed to graduate. Once students successfully complete Stretch English 104/105, they have met the university's First-Year Composition requirement.

Students who choose the stretch option enroll in English 104 in fall and English 105 in spring during their first year at SFSU. Since English 104/105 is a year-long course, students will have the same instructor and group of classmates in the spring semester as they had in the fall semester. The class will also meet at the same day and time during both semesters. This will help when it comes time to plan the rest of your class schedule.

■ *Why Choose Stretch?*

There are at least three benefits to taking Stretch English 104/105 compared to English 114:

Since English 104/105 is a yearlong course, students will have the same instructor and group of classmates in the spring semester as they had in the fall semester.

1. The stretch program allows more time (a full academic year) to meet the learning goals of the course. Because of this extra time, there are more opportunities to practice, to receive and offer feedback, to revise and re-read, before turning in assignments.

2. Stretch English 104/105 has a smaller class size (enrollment is limited to 18 students per class compared to 20 for English 114). This allows students to receive more personal attention, guidance and assistance from their instructor and from their classmates.

3. Students choosing the stretch option earn 6 credits toward the 120 needed for graduation.

DSP and the Composition for Multilingual Students (CMS) Choice

The Composition for Multilingual Students program (CMS) is specifically for students who are nonnative speakers of English. Our CMS program is designed to meet the learning needs of multilingual students, including speech and grammar instruction that is not available in either Stretch English 104/105 or in English 114.

Students who choose the CMS option will be enrolled in the appropriate Level 1 CMS courses at their new student orientation session. For more information about Level 1 CMS courses, please go to http://cmls.sfsu.edu/course-descriptions or email the CMS Coordinator, Lisa Heyer at lheyer@sfsu.edu

■ *Why Choose CMS?*

Even if you did not take ESL classes in high school and you speak English fluently, if English is not your first or primary language, our CMS program may be the most appropriate choice for you for at least three reasons:

1. The CMS Program offers students a comprehensive study of English composition and grammar for those who might otherwise struggle to succeed in the writing courses offered to native speakers of English.

2. CMS Program courses meet the written English requirements for graduation.

3. Completing your writing requirements in the CMS program will not delay your graduation since all the credits earned in CMS courses count toward the 120 units needed for graduation.

How to DSP

San Francisco State University has designed an online application for placing students in first-year composition classes. This application is called Directed Self-Placement (DSP). If your **EPT score is 138–146**, you are **required** to use this application to help you decide which of our three FYC options is best for you.

NOTE

For students with EPT scores LOWER THAN 138, you will complete DSP as part of your Early Start English class. For more information about SFSU's Early Start Program, please go to http://www.sfsu.edu/~advising/esp/home.html.

*If your **EPT score is 138–146**, you are **required** to use this application to help you decide which of our three FYC options is best for you.*

To help you make the best choice possible, you should complete the following steps **before** you access the DSP online application:

Step 1: Carefully read through the DSP Comparison Chart included below, and consider which option best matches your reading and writing abilities. As you consider the questions associated with each option, if *most* of the statements feel true, then that option is a likely good choice.

Step 2: Review the descriptions listed above of the three options (English 114, Stretch English 104/105, or CMS) to confirm your ideas about which course will provide the instruction that best fits your current abilities.

Step 3: Go to the DSP online application at https://dsp.sfsu.edu/.

DSP Comparison Chart

Option 1: The Semester Program	Option 2: The Stretch Program	Option 3: The CMS Program
I think of myself as a strong reader and writer.	I think of myself as an average reader and writer.	In my home growing up, I heard and spoke a language other than English. **AND** I am fluent in spoken English but need more confidence with reading and writing English.
Reading		
• I read actively, taking effective notes as I read, and am comfortable when confronted with difficult texts. • When I read, I make connections to other things I have read or experienced as a means of understanding a reading. • I feel comfortable identifying the structure and organization of the things I read.	• I'm unsure what to do when confronted with difficult texts and unclear about whether or how to take notes. • I only partially understand my reading assignments because I'm not sure how what I read connects to experiences I've had or to other things I've read. • I need to learn about how ideas are related and organized in the readings I do.	• I mainly read in English for school assignments, or to understand an official document. • I only partially understand my reading assignments because I am unfamiliar with important background knowledge and key vocabulary. • I want to develop my vocabulary for college-level English.
Writing		
• I do well finding ideas to write about and I can relate my ideas to the ideas of others. • I have several strategies for brainstorming ideas, outlining, organizing, and revising my writing. • I am confident using the conventions of grammar, punctuation, and spelling.	• I have trouble coming up with good ideas for my essays. • I am unsure of myself when I plan my writing and could use some tips on how to plan, organize, and revise. • I could use some brushing up on grammar and punctuation.	• I write in English mainly for school assignments. • When I write in English, I often don't know how to choose the correct grammar or vocabulary to make my meaning clear. • I need help finding and correcting my grammar and proofreading errors.
Conclusion		
I am ready for college-level reading and writing and to work at a quick pace, with the instructor as my guide. ↓ **English 114**	I would prefer to work at a slower pace with more help from my instructor as I learn to read and write in college. ↓ **Stretch English 104/105**	I would like to complete my first-year composition requirement by taking courses that offer me focused attention on smaller units of the English language including word forms, sentences, and paragraphs ↓ **CMS**

The Online DSP Application

You access the online DSP application at https://dsp.sfsu.edu/. You can complete DSP from your home or at any other convenient location that has internet access. You can also come to SFSU to the English Tutoring Center (ETC) and staff will be there to assist you. The ETC is located in the Humanities Building, Room 290, and will be open Monday through Friday during the summer. You can contact them directly for their specific hours on any given day of the week. They can be reached at their website at https://etc.sfsu.edu, by email at etc@sfsu.edu, or by phone at (415) 338-1821.

Once you access the DSP site, you will see this page. You will log in with your SFSU student identification number and password to begin the DSP process. DSP takes about 3 ½ to 4 hours to complete. You need not complete all the steps at once; you can stop at any point and return later until you complete the process and make your decision about which FYC option is best for you.

After you start the DSP application by logging in with your SFSU ID number and password, you will complete these five steps:

Step 1: Annotate a Reading. In this step, you'll read some tips about how to use annotation to help you understand a short reading. You'll then read and annotate a short selection. This step should take no longer than 1 hour to complete.

Step 2: Plan Your Essay in Response to Reading. This activity is designed to prepare you to write an essay in response to the article you just read and annotated in Step 1. In this step, you'll read some tips about how to read an essay assignment carefully and how to plan an essay based on the reading. This step should take no longer than 40 minutes to complete.

Step 3: Write in Response to a Reading. In this step you will write and upload an essay in response to the reading you did in Step 1. This step should take no longer than 2 hours to complete.

Step 4: Self-Placement Inventory. In this step, you'll be asked to complete a short survey asking you questions about the reading and writing you completed in Steps 1–3. The inventory takes about 10 minutes to complete.

Step 5: Self-Placement Decision. Once you submit your inventory, DSP will take you to the Self-Placement Decision page where, based on your responses to the inventory questions, a recommendation will appear about which FYC option is best for you. You will then be asked to take into consideration your understanding of the difference in the three FYC options, your experience reading the article and writing the essay you just uploaded, how you answered the inventory questions, your past experiences in high school, and any other relevant information to make your final decision about which FYC option is best for you. The final page of DSP looks like this:

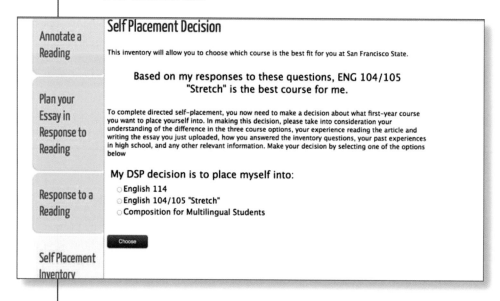

As you can see, once you've considered all the relevant information, you will be asked to make your final choice and select the course you will place yourself into when you attend New Student Orientation. **Be sure to print this final page and bring it with you to your orientation session.**

We understand that 3 ½ to 4 hours is a lot of time and you might be wondering why we are asking you to invest so much time in deciding which FYC course to take. Our experience shows us that when students take the time to think about which course is best for them, they are likely to do better in that course. We want you to succeed at SFSU, and we think the best way to help you succeed is by giving you the time it takes to make this important decision. The time you invest now in picking the right course for you, and then succeeding in that course, is the best possible use of your time.

Registering for FYC Courses During New Student Orientation

During the summer before the Fall 2013 semester begins, incoming students will select a date to attend one of our new student orientation sessions. In addition to lots of helpful information and a chance to visit the campus, a real benefit of attending orientation is that you get to enroll in your FYC course in person during the orientation session. For this reason, it's imperative that you complete DSP **before you attend orientation**.

You must complete DSP no later than the day before the orientation you choose to attend. In order for you to choose the right English course at orientation, you must complete DSP first. If you would like to DSP on campus, you may come to the English Tutoring Center (ETC) the day before orientation, complete DSP, then attend orientation the next day. The ETC is located in the Humanities Building, Room 290 and will be open M–F during the summer. You can contact them directly for their specific hours on any given day of the week. They can be reached at etc@sfsu.edu or (415) 338-1821 or go to their website: https://etc.sfsu.edu.

When you complete DSP, **please print out the final page that shows what FYC program you chose, and bring the decision form to your orientation session**. When you show that printed decision form at orientation, the orientation staff will help you register you in your chosen course.

Students who have not completed DSP will not be allowed to add any classes at orientation. If you have any questions about new student orientation, please contact the Orientation Office by e-mail at orient@sfsu.edu.

You must complete DSP no later than the day before the orientation you choose to attend.

Frequently Asked Questions about DSP

■ *Who is required to DSP?*

If your EPT score is 146–138, you must do the DSP before you can enroll in classes at orientation.

If your EPT score is 137 or lower, you will DSP as part of your **Early Start English** class.

■ *How is DSP administered?*

DSP is an online application. All students log in, and at the conclusion of DSP, select the English course they will take for Fall 2013.

■ *How long does it take to complete DSP?*

DSP can be done in one sitting, or over the course of several days. Plan for 3–4 hours minimum to complete.

■ *What is the cost of DSP?*

DSP is free of charge.

■ *Can I take the DSP at SFSU?*

Yes. The English Tutoring Center has a lab and will be open Monday through Friday. At the lab, students can complete the requirement, and staff will be there to assist students.

■ *How are Orientation and DSP related?*

Students must complete DSP no later than the day before their scheduled orientation session. In order for students to choose the right English course at orientation, they must complete DSP first. Students may come to the English Tutoring Center the day before orientation, finish DSP, then attend orientation the next day. ***Students who have not completed DSP will not be allowed to add any classes at orientation***.

■ *Once I've completed DSP, can I change my mind?*

No. Because such changes would present enormous challenges for students and the university alike, it will not be possible once the semester begins for you to change your DSP choice. For this reason, it is best for you to weigh your options carefully before you complete the DSP.

4

What to Expect from FYC

Regardless of which FYC option you choose, we want you to be successful. Besides attending class regularly and doing all of the assigned work to the best of your ability, there are a number of things you can do to help yourself succeed in your FYC course.

Expect Something Different from High School

Since many, if not most, of you will be going into your chosen FYC course right out of high school, a good place to start is to expect that your FYC course will be different from the English classes you took in high school. The tables that follow will help you learn what some of those differences are and to adjust your expectations accordingly.[1]

. . . expect that your FYC course will be different from the English classes you took in high school.

You must balance your responsibilities and set priorities.

How is College Different from High School? 1	
Following the Rules in High School	**Choosing Responsibly in College**
High school is mandatory and usually free.	College is voluntary and expensive.
Your time is structured by others.	You manage your own time.
You need permission to participate in extra-curricular activities.	You must decide whether to participate in cocurricular activities.
You can count on parents and teachers to remind you of your responsibilities and guide you in setting priorities.	You must balance your responsibilities and set priorities. You will face moral and ethical decisions you have never faced before.
Each day you proceed from one class directly to another, spending 6 hours each day—30 hours a week—in class.	You often have hours between classes; class times vary throughout the day and evening and you spend only 12 to 16 hours each week in class.
Most of your classes are arranged for you.	You arrange your own schedule in consultation with your advisor. Schedules tend to look lighter than they really are.
You are not responsible for knowing what it takes to graduate.	Graduation requirements are complex, and differ from year to year. You are expected to know those that apply to you.
Guiding principle: You will usually be told what to do and corrected if your behavior is out of line.	**Guiding principle:** You are expected to take responsibility for what you do and don't do, as well as for the consequences of your decisions.

[1]Tables used with permission from the Altshuler Learning Enhancement Center at Southern Methodist University <http://smu.edu/alec/tranisition.asp>.

How is College Different from High School?　2

Going to High School Classes	Succeeding in College Classes
The school year is 36 weeks long; some classes extend over both semesters and some don't.	The academic year is divided into two separate 15-week semesters, plus a week after each semester for exams.
Classes generally have no more than 35 students.	Classes may number 100 students or more.
You may study outside class as little as 0 to 2 hours a week, and this may be mostly last-minute test preparation.	You need to study at least 2 to 3 hours outside of class for each hour in class.
You seldom need to read anything more than once, and sometimes listening in class is enough.	You need to review class notes and text material regularly.
You are expected to read short assignments that are then discussed, and often re-taught, in class.	You are assigned substantial amounts of reading and writing that may not be directly addressed in class.
Guiding principle: You will usually be told in class what you need to learn from assigned reading.	**Guiding principle:** College is a learning environment in which you take responsibility for thinking through and applying what you have learned.

How is College Different from High School?　3

High School Teachers	College Professors
Teachers check your completed homework.	Professors may not always check completed homework, but they will assume you can perform the same tasks on tests.
Teachers remind you of your incomplete work.	Professors may not remind you of incomplete work.
Teachers approach you if they believe you need assistance.	Professors are usually open and helpful, but most expect you to initiate contact if you need assistance.
Teachers are often available for conversation before, during, or after class.	Professors expect and want you to attend their scheduled office hours.
Teachers have been trained in teaching methods to assist in imparting knowledge to students.	Professors have been trained as experts in their particular areas of research.
Teachers provide you with information you missed when you were absent.	Professors expect you to get from classmates any notes from classes you missed.
Teachers present material to help you understand the material in the textbook.	Professors may not follow the textbook. Instead, to amplify the text, they may give illustrations, provide background information, or discuss research about the topic you are studying. Or they may expect you to relate the classes to the textbook readings.

Teachers often write information on the board to be copied in your notes.	Professors may lecture nonstop, expecting you to identify the important points in your notes. When professors write on the board, it may be to amplify the lecture, not to summarize it. Good notes are a must.
Teachers impart knowledge and facts, sometimes drawing direct connections and leading you through the thinking process.	Professors expect you to think about and synthesize seemingly unrelated topics.
Teachers often take time to remind you of assignments and due dates.	Professors expect you to read, save, and consult the course syllabus (outline); the syllabus spells out exactly what is expected of you, when it is due, and how you will be graded.
Teachers carefully monitor class attendance.	Professors may not formally take roll, but they are still likely to know whether or not you attended.
Guiding principle: High school is a teaching environment in which you acquire facts and skills.	**Guiding principle:** College is a learning environment in which you take responsibility for thinking through and applying what you have learned.

How is College Different from High School? 4

Tests in High School	Tests in College
Testing is frequent and covers small amounts of material.	Testing is usually infrequent and may be cumulative, covering large amounts of material. You, not the professor, need to organize the material to prepare for the test. A particular course may have only 2 or 3 tests in a semester.
Makeup tests are often available.	Makeup tests are seldom an option; if they are, you need to request them.
Teachers frequently rearrange test dates to avoid conflict with school events.	Professors in different courses usually schedule tests without regard to the demands of other courses or outside activities.
Teachers frequently conduct review sessions, pointing out the most important concepts.	Professors rarely offer review sessions, and when they do, they expect you to be an active participant, one who comes prepared with questions.
Guiding principle: Mastery is usually seen as the ability to reproduce what you were taught in the form in which it was presented to you, or to solve the kinds of problems you were shown how to solve.	**Guiding principle:** Mastery is often seen as the ability to apply what you've learned to new situations or to solve new kinds of problems.

How is College Different from High School?	5
Grades in High School	**Grades in College**
Grades are given for most assigned work.	Grades may not be provided for all assigned work.
Consistently good homework grades may raise your overall grade when test grades are low.	Grades on tests and major papers usually provide most of the course grade.
Extra credit projects are often available to help you raise your grade.	Grades on tests and major papers usually provide most of the course grade.
Initial test grades, especially when they are low, may not have an adverse effect on your final grade.	Watch out for your first tests. These are usually "wake-up calls" to let you know what is expected—but they also may account for a substantial part of your course grade. You may be shocked when you get your grades.
You may graduate as long as you have passed all required courses with a grade of D or higher.	You may graduate only if your average in classes meets the departmental standard—typically a 2.0 or C.
Guiding principle: Effort counts. Courses are usually structured to reward a "good-faith effort."	**Guiding principle:** Results count. Though "good-faith effort" is important in regard to the professor's willingness to help you achieve good results, it will not substitute for results in the grading process.

"Good-faith effort" . . . will not substitute for results in the grading process.

How to Succeed in FYC

Now that you can better adjust your expectations for FYC, we think you'll find the following tips helpful to your success in FYC. Some of this information is taken up in greater detail in other chapters of this guide.

■ *Seven Tips for Success*

1. **Promptly acquire all required course materials.** On the first day of class, your instructor will inform you of all the required materials for the course (these will usually also be stated on the syllabus). To succeed in your course, you will need to get these materials as quickly as possible. If you have any difficulty obtaining any of the required materials, let your instructor know as soon as possible.

2. **Be mindful of the University Class Attendance Policy,** which generally states that students are expected to attend classes regularly because classroom work is one of the necessary and important means of learning and

of attaining the educational objectives of the institution. In Chapter 7, "Policies and Procedures," we cover the university and FYC attendance policy in fuller detail.

3. **Be a courteous and responsible member of the classroom community.** One of the greatest benefits of being in college is the classroom community. At its best, this community will provide you with support, knowledge, and a place to develop with others who are learning alongside you. In an FYC class, in particular, this community will offer you plenty of opportunities to develop your academic reading and writing skills. Each class will be filled with language—with writing, discussion, reading, and listening—so if you miss a day of class, you miss a great deal of work. In our experience, students who attend class every day are more likely to pass the class.

4. **Successfully collaborate with peers.** To ensure that this community works to your benefit, your instructor will ask you to observe some common ground rules for class participation. Knowing when to ask questions, knowing how to work with others, knowing how to contribute, knowing how to listen and speak—ultimately, knowing how to be a member of the college classroom will be key to your success. Typically, some common ground rules include:

   - Turning off all cell phones and any other electronic equipment during class time or, if your instructor permits, using only for appropriate class purposes

   - Being respectful of your classmates' ideas (no matter what your personal opinion of those ideas might be!)

   - Coming to class prepared, having read and done the assigned work to the best of your ability

   - Participating actively in whole class and small group discussions, asking questions, offering ideas, volunteering assistance

   - And in general, doing your best to contribute to the learning process, rather than disrupt it.

5. **Be a civil and responsible member of the campus community.** Students are expected to be civil to one another and to others in the campus community, and contribute positively to student and university life. In Chapter 7, "Policies and Procedures," we describe the university's policy on student conduct.

6. **Meet your instructor in office hours and conferences.** Making appointments to meet with your instructor one-on-one during his/her office hours is

Making appointments to meet with your instructor one-on-one during his/her office hours is an excellent opportunity for you to get individual help . . .

an excellent opportunity for you to get individual help with an assignment, to clarify any questions you might have about an assignment, and/or to help you set individual goals to help you be successful. Your instructor will inform you in class, and will state on the syllabus, what times he/she is available for office hour appointments. Your instructor might also distribute a sign-up sheet in class for individual conferences. Whether your instructor provides a sign-up sheet, or you make an appointment to meet with him/her on your own, meeting with your instructor outside of class during office hours is an important resource to help you succeed in college. See Chapter 6 for more information about meeting with your instructor.

7. **Take advantage of the academic support services available to you.** If you or your instructor thinks you might benefit from some supplemental instruction and/or other assistance, he or she can make a referral to one of our several campus support services. You can also seek out these support services on your own. These services are described in Chapter 6, "FYC Resources and Academic Support."

Top Ten Excuses (that Just Won't Work) for Missing Class or Not Turning in Assignments[2]

Just as using the suggested tips can help you succeed in FYC, there are also some things you can do that are guaranteed to cause trouble. We list them here, hoping you'll avoid them like the plague. And remember, there is no excuse you can come up with that we haven't already heard a thousand times before.

1. **I overslept.**
    Alarm clock? Earlier bedtime? Later class? Rig a bucket of ice water to your alarm?

2. **My computer died/I saved it to the wrong device/the file won't open/my printer ran out of ink.**
    The strangest things seem to happen to homework assignments and essays, so it is always a good idea to save frequently, print a copy, and/or save a copy to external media (like a flash drive) or to a cloud-based server. Oh yes, and make sure that it has actually saved properly before you shut down the computer. Be sure to keep an extra ink cartridge on hand or know places on campus that have printers you can use. See Chapter 8 for the location and hours for various computer labs on campus.

---

[2]Adapted with permission from *Composing Yourself: A Student Guide to Introductory Composition at Purdue*, 2012–2013, pgs. 29–30.

3. **I was sick … so sick I couldn't even e-mail.**
We are delighted you are feeling well enough to rejoin the class and that you are no longer contagious … you're not, right? It's always a good idea to contact your instructor as soon as you realize you are going to miss class due to illness. And it's useful to bring a detailed physician's note to class if you've missed more than a couple of days. Our absence policy is listed in Chapter 7 of this guide and will also be on the class syllabus.

4. **There was a family emergency/death in the family.**
We are sorry for your loss and you have our deepest sympathy, but the university has a standard policy for absences.

5. **I didn't get the assignment/I didn't know the due date/I didn't understand what we were supposed to do.**
All assignments and due dates are listed on the class syllabus and typically on iLearn as well. If all else fails, you can always call upon your classmates or your instructor for assistance.

6. **I was studying for another class.**
Uh huh.

7. **I forgot what day I had class/conferences. I forgot which room we were in.**
Remember the handy calendar your instructor suggested you fill out? Now's the time to get it out and use it.

8. **I lost my keys. I got locked out of my car/dorm room/apartment.**
A little notification goes a long way. If some such misfortune befalls you, just take a second (while waiting for maintenance or a locksmith) to give your instructor a call or send her an e-mail. If you have something due you can also submit it electronically so as not to have it be too terribly late. But first be sure to check with your instructor about her policy on electronic submissions.

9. **My roommate is having a really difficult time right now.**
There are many resources available on campus for students struggling with a variety of issues. See Chapter 10 of this guide where we list these resources and refer your roommate to them.

10. **I couldn't do the homework because I don't have my book yet.**
In the rare case where the book is out of stock at the campus bookstore or you just haven't been able to buy it yet, it is still your responsibility to keep up with the readings in your FYC course. You can borrow the book from a classmate, talk to your instructor, see if the library has a copy, or see if you

In the rare case where the book is out of stock at the campus bookstore or you just haven't been able to buy it yet, it is still your responsibility to keep up with the readings in your FYC course.

can purchase a less expensive copy from an online retailer. Falling behind in the reading at the beginning of the semester never works out well in the end.

Participation in FYC: What Will be Expected of Me?

Much of the work of the FYC classroom is collaborative. You are therefore expected to attend class, prepared and ready to participate in the community of the classroom. (Now might be a good time to review those "Seven Tips for Success" in FYC!). Your FYC instructor will state in his syllabus the specific grading policy for class participation and how much it will factor into your final grade.

■ *In-Class Discussions*

There are two general kinds of in-class discussions to which you'll contribute in your FYC class: discussions about reading and discussions about writing. The reading discussions require you to come to class having done the reading, ready to ask questions and to offer your responses to the reading as the class works together to discover what is meaningful in the text. Your class will also discuss how the reading serves as a model for your own writing.

The writing discussions require you to come to class ready to share your writing with your classmates and to offer your classmates thoughtful responses to their writing. These writing discussions are described more thoroughly in Chapter 5 in the sections on Peer Review and Writing Workshop and Writer's Chair.

Participation in class discussions affects not only your grade, but also helps you become a better reader and writer. These discussions often cannot be "made up" if you miss class on the day they take place; therefore, regular class attendance is crucial.

■ *Group Work*

Because of the social nature of reading and writing (and because it's generally true that "two heads are better than one"), you will also be expected to participate in a number of small group activities. In addition to Peer Review, your instructor may also have you work in reading groups (or Book Clubs), give group presentations, or participate in debates of key issues that come up in the readings (and this is only a small sampling of the kinds of group activities that take place in FYC).

Group work, whether planned in advance or impromptu, also helps you to become a better reader/writer and will also affect your grade in the class. Like

The reading discussions require you to come to class having done the reading, ready to ask questions and to offer your responses to the reading . . .

The writing discussions require you to come to class ready to share your writing with your classmates and to offer your classmates thoughtful responses to their writing.

Because of the social nature of reading and writing (and because it's generally true that "two heads are better than one"), you will also be expected to participate in a number of small group activities.

class discussions, group work also cannot be easily "made up" if you are absent. So once again, regular attendance is key!

■ *Online Discussions and Group Work*

In addition to in-class discussions and group work, you can expect that your instructor will also ask you to participate in online activities. We describe some of the more typical online activities in Chapter 8.

Top Ten Reasons to Take (and Enjoy) your FYC Course[3]

Much will be expected of you in your FYC class. But you can also expect to get much from it. Here are ten good reasons to take FYC. Enjoy!

1. **You'll have a small class size.**
    You'll have no more than 18 or 20 students in your FYC class. You'll get to know them and their writing quite well. You may or may not meet your new "BFF," but at least you'll know the names of at least 18–20 other freshmen who are going through the same adjustment to college life that you are.

2. **Your instructor will know your name.**
    With such a small number of students, your instructor will know your name and you will know your classmates' names as well. Your instructor will also have time to meet you in office hours if you'd like to talk about your work outside of class.

3. **Your composition instructor is a pretty good resource.**
    Need a letter of recommendation for Study Abroad? A scholarship? Can't figure out how to organize your paper for history class? Need a job and don't have a résumé? Need to know the best place on campus to get a slice of pizza? Ask your instructor. If he can't help you, he can direct you to someone who can.

4. **You'll learn a ton about reading and writing in college.**
    Whether you read or wrote a lot or a little in high school, you'll find that reading and writing in college and outside the university requires you to adapt to new rhetorical situations, compose in new genres, and to integrate multiple media. Don't worry if "rhetorical situations," "new genres" and "multiple media" sound unfamiliar. That just means that our FYC courses are the right place for you!

---

[3]Adapted with permission from *Composing Yourself: A Student Guide to Introductory Composition at Purdue*, 2012–2013, pgs. 32–33.

5. **If you are already a good writer, your composition course could be a GPA boost!**

   Even if you did well in your high school English classes, you need to continue to read and write in order to hone your skills. The reading and writing you did in high school was prep work for what you'll do now.

6. **You'll get to practice, practice, practice!**

   Do you play basketball? Play guitar? Knit? You have to practice to improve your skills, right? The same is true for reading and writing. To improve, you have to read and write often. FYC gives you the opportunity to practice and improve with instruction and feedback from your instructor and classmates.

7. **You'll learn about composition in a whole new way.**

   You'll learn to produce a variety of texts—for your FYC class, you might be creating films, books, comics, games, articles, websites or reports that go beyond the typical essay. In the process, you'll also learn how to analyze these texts in rhetorically sound ways and to think about how they operate in a larger social context.

8. **You'll learn about the University libraries at SFSU.**

   You might take a field trip to visit the J. Paul Leonard and Sutro Libraries, or the Labor Archives and Research Center. You might learn about information retrieval and the numerous databases you have access to through the Leonard Library. Our library is new and, in addition to a computer lab that is open 24 hours a day, it has a nice Peet's Coffee shop and comfortable places to sit and study.

9. **You'll take your writing and reading skills with you.**

   You'll learn to write for different audiences, in different genres, with different media. Whatever you learn, you'll be able to transfer it to your other classes. Not only will the next-level composition class (ENG 214), build directly on what you learned in FYC, but you will take this learning with you to into your major. See Chapter 9, "What Comes After FYC."

10. **You'll use and improve your technology skills.**

    Not all compositions are written on 8 ½ by 11 paper. You might use your composing skills to create a webpage, a podcast, a brochure, blog or short video. You may learn to use software you've never tried before. Either way, you'll learn about visual rhetoric and how visuals impact your communication.

5

Your Writing and FYC

Revision

Peer Review and Collaborative Writing

Writing Workshop and Writer's Chair

Feedback

Portfolios

Permission to Use Student Work

FYC is a place where your writing— and how you can continue to develop and hone your writing skills—will be taken seriously.

Although you'll read a variety of texts in FYC, perhaps the most important text you'll work with is your own writing. FYC is a place where your writing—and how you can continue to develop and hone your writing skills—will be taken seriously. You should keep all copies of your drafts and bring all of your writing to every class—from freewrites in your notebook, to drafts with feedback, to working revisions. You will regularly be asked to take out a piece of writing and work on it, applying class lessons, strategizing for revision, or discussing your work with peers or your instructor. You'll frequently be asked to collaborate with your peers, giving and receiving constructive feedback. Whether working on revising your writing, engaging in peer review, or collecting your work in a final portfolio, FYC will give you many opportunities to grow and develop as a writer.

Revision

A good deal of learning about writing, reading, and thinking is being able to see your own work and ideas with fresh eyes . . .

All FYC classes stress revision, in terms of reading and writing and in terms of thinking. For writers, revision is an inseparable part of the writing process; writing is much more than initial thoughts and initial drafts. Revision gives you a chance to return to your first ideas closely and critically and re-see or re-imagine beyond your initial ideas and impressions. A good deal of learning about writing, reading, and thinking is being able to see your own work and ideas with fresh eyes, determining what it does and doesn't achieve, and then seeing where you might go from where you are now.

But what does revision mean, exactly? In FYC, we take the word revision literally to mean re-viewing, re-reading, re-thinking, and re-writing. Re-vision happens whenever you reread, rewrite, or rethink in order to deepen your understanding. You will be encouraged to use the revision process to improve both your reading and writing—generating new insights, taking new points of view into account, and authoring new writing that shows the elaboration and deepening of your thinking.

You will be encouraged to use the revision process to improve both your reading and writing—generating new insights, taking new points of view into account . . .

This is quite a different view of revision than just editing, proofreading, or "cleaning up" your earlier draft. Instead, you will be asked to use feedback and your own rereading and rewriting processes as opportunities to go back to your first impressions and see where you might further develop the ideas you find there. Likewise, revision offers the chance to work on really crafting and fine-tuning your writing so you can be as effective a writer as possible.

Peer Review and Collaborative Writing

All FYC classes will make use of peer review throughout the term. Peer review is a hallmark of academic writing at every level. Just like scholars and scientists rely on peer review to ensure their ideas are sound, so too will you rely on peer review to test your ideas and to ensure you've communicated those ideas clearly and effectively.

Central to our method of peer review is responding as an engaged reader. This means you won't typically be asked to "correct" a peer's work. Instead, you will be asked to use the same reading skills and strategies you use on published texts to read one another's writing. By acting as an engaged reader (or audience) for your peers' work, you can help other writers in your class deepen their thinking by asking questions, mirroring back to writers what you think they are saying in their written work, or pointing out places in their texts where you were confused or needed more information. Later in the writing process, your instructor might ask you to read one another's work for organization, rhetorical strategies, sentence structures, or other lessons you've been working on.

Whenever you practice peer review, it's important to remember that the benefits are actually a two-way street. Although you're offering solid insights and an engaged response to your peer's work, you simultaneously get the benefit of honing your own critical reading skills. You should think of every peer review as an opportunity to practice the very same lessons you'll need to apply to your own writing.

Some obvious guidelines for peer review are worth mentioning here. First, your responses should always be generous and respectful—think about what feedback will genuinely help the writer most at this particular stage of the writing process. Ask questions. Offer how you were affected as a reader of the text—where were you most interested and where did you get a bit lost?

Next, even as you are being respectful, you do want to offer substantial, thoughtful, and specific feedback. Just telling a writer "This is good" or "This doesn't flow" won't go very far in helping that writer address the problem or replicate a successful strategy. Try to explain exactly why or how you felt the way you did: a statement like "this part really worked because you gave a concrete image I could connect to" is much more helpful to the writer. Try to discuss specific places in the text where you encountered something excellent or something that needs work. Remember that if you're not sure about an idea or part of the essay, you can always ask the writer a question and try to puzzle through what would work better together. Two heads are often better than one!

Writing Workshop and Writer's Chair

In addition to the ways peer review puts your writing at the center of the class, many FYC classes will also make use of writing workshops or a writer's chair activity to help you focus specifically on how you can improve your writing. In a workshop, your instructor might make copies of your essay or copy excerpts

> *You should think of every peer review as an opportunity to practice the very same lessons you'll need to apply to your own writing.*

from several essays, often with names removed, to begin a discussion about effective writing. Or, your instructor might ask students to take turns in "the writer's chair" where the class examines your writing and offers suggestions for how to make it stronger.

Although the writer in these situations gets valuable feedback, everyone gains tremendously from this experience, since you are learning and practicing how to read a piece of writing with a critical eye and discussing together how to make writing more effective. Similar to peer review, practicing your critical reading skills on others' writing will thus help you with the much harder task of revising your own writing with a critical eye. It will also help you develop a language for talking about writing with others.

> *. . . practicing your critical reading skills on others' writing will thus help you with the much harder task of revising your own writing with a critical eye.*

Feedback

In FYC, your instructor takes your writing seriously and she wants to help you become a stronger, more adept writer. As one of the many ways you will practice improving your writing, then, your instructor will offer you substantial feedback on much of your written work. For some of you, this feedback might seem different than responses you've received in the past in that your instructor will focus not just on mechanics (grammar, spelling, formatting or citation) but also on your ideas and arguments.

You should therefore expect your instructor to ask questions and respond to the content of your writing as well as to the style of the writing itself. In this way, your instructor is also helping you acclimate to the thinking and understanding expected at the college level; she will inevitably ask you to test your ideas, to dig deeper, and to provide more evidence for your arguments. Responding in this way is crucial, because as we know, successful writing not only says something well, but has something worth saying.

> *You should therefore expect your instructor to ask questions and respond to the content of your writing as well as to the style of the writing itself.*

It is worth noting that while feedback from your instructor will be a key tool to help you strengthen your writing, the feedback you receive from two other parties is also vitally important: your peers and yourself. We've discussed peer review and its importance above, but it's important to stress again that the peer review process will also help you become a better reader of your own work. Throughout the term, you will often be called upon to use "self-assessment," or your own ability to reread your writing carefully and critically and assess how effective it is. In this way, you can offer yourself useful feedback, in addition to the responses you receive from other readers.

Portfolios

Our FYC program uses a portfolio system to review and grade your work. At the end of the semester, and perhaps at other designated times throughout the term, your instructor will ask you to select and revise samples of your work to submit as a portfolio.

Portfolio grading has many benefits for students. Students are able to apply feedback and revise work before submitting portfolios, and since portfolios are collected at the end of the term they give students more time to practice writing strategies and skills before they are evaluated. Portfolios thus give you a chance to thoughtfully select your best work that represents you as a writer, as well as to allow you the chance to demonstrate your growth as a writer over time.

You might be wondering what the portfolio grading system means in terms of receiving grades and feedback. Often this means that your instructor may give you feedback on earlier drafts instead of a grade. This will allow you to stay focused on your writing and how to improve; it can also allow you to take more substantial risks in your writing—trying out new ideas and new ways of articulating those ideas—since you won't have to worry about receiving a grade until you submit your portfolio. Since you are adjusting to college and perhaps new expectations for your writing, the portfolio system gives you more room to explore and develop your ideas and writing before you are evaluated. If at any time one of your assignments does not meet the basic requirements and expectations (i.e., it would receive a failing grade) your instructor will let you know.

Portfolios emphasize three things: **choice**, **variety**, and **reflection**. **Choice** means that you have some choice (sometimes within guidelines) about the work you select to include in your portfolio. **Variety** means that you will choose a variety of written work—shorter to longer essays, different types of writing (or genres), and work from across the semester—to represent your learning for the term. And **reflection** means that you will be asked to reflect on your learning and your writing, often analyzing your own growth and how the work you selected for your portfolio demonstrates what you have learned.

In short, portfolios give you the opportunity to realize what you have learned and to put your best foot forward in presenting your work. Portfolios also give your instructor a way to understand you as a writer more holistically (instead of in terms of a single paper). Finally, portfolios allow you and your instructor to assess whether you've met the learning outcomes for the course.

Your final portfolio should include the following:

- A reflective introduction to the portfolio. Your introduction will frame your work for your readers, reflect on the specific strengths of the work you've included, and reflect on your growth as a student, reader, and writer.

- An example of analytical or persuasive writing. In higher education, we value the ability to analyze ideas and texts. This means both thinking

Portfolios thus give you a chance to thoughtfully select your best work . . .

. . . the portfolio system gives you more room to explore and develop your ideas and writing before being evaluated.

. . . portfolios give you the opportunity to realize what you have learned and to put your best foot forward in presenting your work.

In higher education, we value the ability to analyze ideas and texts.

critically about ideas or perspectives (including those new or different from your own) and thinking rhetorically about how texts are put together, how they work, and how they affect readers. **Analysis** often means breaking things down to see how they work, to gain greater understanding, and ultimately to offer your own thoughts in return. This is where persuasion comes in—once you've used analysis to come to a greater understanding, how can you persuade others to accept your ideas or perspective? **Persuasion** often relies on both analytical and logical facts (or logos), as well as emotional reasons or support (or pathos). To be persuasive, you must also think carefully about how you present yourself as an informed writer (ethos), as well as how to best communicate to your chosen audience. You will practice analysis and persuasion in your FYC class; your portfolio will contain one sample of this dimension of your writing.

■ An example of research-based writing. As you know, one of the primary goals of a university is to conduct research, as well as to teach students how to research for themselves. **Research** is happening any time you ask a question and seek information to answer that question. Research can mean talking to experts or involved parties, using the library to find reliable information, conducting ethnographic research where you observe a group or event, or even using (and sifting through) the vast amount of information available on the internet. In FYC you'll practice making a research plan: from asking a good question, to finding information, to judging the quality of that information, and finally, to using that information to support your own ideas.

■ A third longer essay which demonstrates your strengths or your growth as a writer.

One of your essays may fulfill more than one of the items above—for example, you might have an essay that is both analytical and research-based. The point of the portfolio is to collect a range of your writing so that you can provide a clear picture of your work in FYC. In addition to the above materials, your instructor may also ask you to include samples of the short assignments you've completed, peer reviews, or other homework/responses. Your instructor will give you specific guidelines about anything he or she would like you to include and help you to create a strong portfolio showcasing your work.

Permission to Use Student Work

As you learn various models of academic writing in your FYC, chances are you will find it helpful to see examples of student work to use as models. As collaboration is also at the core of the FYC course you may be asked by your

> *Research is happening any time you ask a question and seek information to answer that question.*

instructor to allow the use of your own writing as part of a helpful lesson for you and the rest of the class. Most students find this to be a valuable and non-threatening aspect of the first year composition classroom, which helps them become more comfortable workshopping and revising their own—and their classmates'—writing.

Typically, at the start of the semester your instructor will ask you to sign a "Permission to Use Student Work" form (see next page). Signing this form means you are allowing your instructor to use your work as an example in class or in research. The use of student work in class is a helpful teaching tool, and your writing can be used anonymously if you prefer. You are not obligated to sign this form, and in no way can your grade in the class be affected should you chose not to sign.

As collaboration is also at the core of the FYC course you may be asked by your instructor to allow the use of your own writing as part of a helpful lesson for you and the rest of the class.

Permission to Use Student Work

Dear Student,

Because it is helpful to the class to use examples of student work during teaching, I am asking your permission to reproduce the writing you do this semester. If you grant me permission, there are several ways I might use your work:

- I may make copies or transparencies of your work to use as an example during a class lesson, either this semester or in a future semester.

- I may use it as an example in a Course Reader or a textbook sometime in the future.

- I might post part or the entire whole of your paper as an example on the class website.

- I might quote a passage of your writing in a conference paper or article in a professional journal.

Of course, it is also possible that I won't use your work at all, even if you give me permission to.

You are free to chose not to allow me to use your work, and if this is your decision in no way will your grade be negatively affected in my course. If you decide to allow me to use your work, please check the appropriate boxes on the following page and return it to me. If you decide to grant me permission to use your writing, you may withdraw that permission at any time or for any assignment.

Thank you for your consideration!

_____

(Instructor Signature)

Student Permission Form

To: _____

    (Instructor's Name)

You have my permission to use my writing from this course as examples in this or future writing courses, teaching workshops, professional publications, and/or Course Readers/Textbooks.

Please check one of the following:

_____ You may use my first and last name to identify my work.

_____ You may use my first name only.

_____ You may use my work, but not my name.

Student Signature: _____

Printed Name: _____

Date: _____

Course, Section, CRN: _____

6

FYC Resources and Academic Support

Yes, we expect a lot from you in FYC, but never fear; we also offer you a lot of support. Here, we list some of the most important resources available to you. Making use of these resources is a virtual guarantee that you'll find your experience in FYC to be rewarding and productive (and even enjoyable!)

Your Course Instructor

Every instructor has at least one hour a week set aside for drop-in office hours.

When you are a student in a first-year composition course, your instructor is your most important resource. Every instructor has at least one hour a week set aside for drop-in office hours. Office hours and your instructor's office location will be listed on your syllabus, and your instructor will post her office hours outside her office. Make sure you note the location of your instructor's office—unlike many high school teachers, college instructors do not have their offices in the rooms they teach in. If you forget the location of your instructor's office, you can always check one of the directories in the Humanities building:

- College of Liberal and Creative Arts faculty directories are posted on the large bulletin boards across from the elevator on the north side of the building on both the first and second floor.

- A directory of Composition faculty and staff is posted on the bulletin board next to the Composition department office in HUM 209.

Every first-year composition instructor has a mailbox in HUM 125.

Your instructor will also include an e-mail contact and a phone number on her syllabus, and will explain the best ways to contact her. Also, every first-year composition instructor has a mailbox in HUM 125. All of the mailboxes are arranged alphabetically by last name. If you need help or have a question about the class or an assignment, contact your instructor. Just remember to check the course syllabus/assignment sheet/course website first, to see if you can find the information you need there—being respectful of the value of others' time is an important part of being a successful student and professional.

If your instructor has to cancel class, she'll call in to her department to let them know, and a sign will be posted outside the door to notify students. If she can, your instructor will also contact you ahead of time via e-mail. If your instructor does not show up by 15 minutes after the time class was supposed to begin and no notice has been posted outside your classroom door, check your e-mail or the course website to see if your instructor has left a cancellation message. If you don't have internet access or have checked and found no message, visit the Composition Department office in HUM 209 and ask if the instructor has cancelled class. If the Composition office is closed, you can inquire at the English Department office in HUM 289.

NOTE

Has your class been cancelled? Check the cancellation notice carefully; first of all, you want to make sure the cancellation notice is for **your** class, not another section that happens to meet in the same room. Once you've verified that it is your class that has been cancelled, look for more details. Often, instructors will include a brief note about homework or other activities they expect you to complete by the next class meeting. Check your e-mail to see if your instructor has contacted you about the cancellation. If your class has a course iLearn site or other website, check to see if further instructions have been posted there.

If your instructor cancels class repeatedly, or fails to show up for class meetings, contact the Composition Department office by visiting HUM 209 or calling (415) 338-2128.

If you have a conflict with your instructor, or have a question or concern about the class that you do not feel comfortable bringing to your instructor's attention, contact first-year composition coordinator Dr. Tara Lockhart at (415) 338-1711, or via e-mail at taralock@sfsu.edu. She will put you in contact with the person who can best address your questions or concerns.

■ *Office hour etiquette*

- First of all, visit office hours! Students who do tend to be more successful than students who don't. Use office hours to ask your instructor that question you didn't want to ask in class. Ask your instructor if you can bring in a draft to get feedback before an essay is due. It's okay even to just stop by to say hi, or talk about writing you're doing for other classes.

- If another student is already meeting with your instructor, wave hi so that your instructor knows you are waiting to see her, and then step out into the hallway to give the other student some privacy while they finish their meeting.

- Don't expect your instructor to be available to chat any time she's in her office; posted office hours are definitely set aside for your instructor to meet with you, but at other times, she may be busy prepping for her next class.

Tutoring Centers

The on-campus tutoring centers are a fantastic free resource for students, and every first-year composition instructor can tell you that students who

The on-campus tutoring centers are a fantastic free resource for students . . .

take advantage of these resources are far more likely to pass the class, not to mention more likely to earn a good grade. The English Tutoring Center (ETC) and Learning Assistance Center (LAC) will be especially valuable to you, as they both offer tutoring designed specifically for students in FYC courses.

■ *Tutoring Referrals*

Your instructor will probably ask you to provide a sample of your writing in the first few days of class, which he'll then evaluate to get a sense of what needs you might have as a writer. If your instructor sees a need for it, he may then give you a referral for weekly tutoring at one of the campus tutoring centers. If you get one of these tutoring referrals, take it! Weekly tutoring with an experienced tutor will help you:

- Stay on track with your assignments.

- Ensure that you understand your assignments fully and are completing them as instructed.

- Develop study habits that will help you succeed in college.

- Develop reading and writing strategies that will help you succeed in your first-year composition class and beyond.

And all at the low, low cost of **absolutely free**. You may even be able to earn a unit of credit for your weekly tutoring sessions (ask when you enroll at the tutoring center).

If your instructor doesn't refer you to weekly tutoring, that doesn't mean you don't need it or won't benefit from it. You are welcome to ask your instructor for a tutoring referral. (Most instructors are impressed when students show this kind of initiative.) Tell your instructor what you want to focus on in tutoring, so that he can provide a referral that explains your particular goals.

Although each tutoring center has its own referral form and procedures, the steps you take as a student are pretty much the same: visit the tutoring center with your referral and a sample of your writing. Your instructor will tell you the deadline for signing up for weekly tutoring. It's best to sign up as early as you can, so that you have the best chance of getting your preferred tutoring schedule. The tutoring center will have you fill out an intake form, which will tell them both what you want to get out of tutoring, and what days and times work best for you. As soon as the center finds a tutor who can work with you at one of the days and times you've requested, they'll let you know.

■ *Getting the Most out of Tutoring*

To make the most of your tutoring appointments, whether you have dedicated weekly appointments or just drop in to work on a particular assignment, follow these tips:

- ■ Make your appointments in advance to get tutoring at the times that are most convenient for you.

- ■ When you go to your appointment, bring the assignment sheet for the assignment you want to work on, plus any handouts and readings your tutor will need to understand the assignment. Also bring along any other materials you'll need to complete it successfully, such as assigned readings, or, in the case of a research-based assignment, sources you've found that you plan to draw upon in your writing.

- ■ Arrive on time for your appointment. Make sure you schedule your appointments so that you can arrive on time and stay until the end.

- ■ Have a specific goal in mind for each appointment.

- ■ If you're not sure what your next goal should be, ask your instructor for suggestions. He knows your writing and will be able to make helpful suggestions when you are trying to set tutoring priorities.

When you go to your appointment, bring the assignment sheet for the assignment you want to work on . . .

Tutoring is a great opportunity to get to know a fellow student who has had years of experience navigating college life. The tutors you'll be working with are usually graduate or upper-division students, and many of the graduate students tutoring first-year composition students are themselves studying to teach first-year composition.

Tutoring Centers for FYC

English Tutoring Center (ETC)	Coordinator: James Warren Boyd Staff Director: Jessica Morrow	(415) 338-1821 etc@sfsu.edu https://etc.sfsu.edu	HUM 290

As the name suggests, the English Tutoring Center (ETC) is the tutoring center run by the English Department. Weekly tutoring sign-ups are at the beginning of the semester. One-time appointments are also available throughout the semester: sign up for one by calling or e-mailing the ETC, or stop by and sign up for a spot using the appointment binder.

Learning Assistance Center (LAC)	Director: Deborah vanDommelen	(415) 338-1993 lac@sfsu.edu https://www.sfsu.edu/~lac/	HSS 348

The Learning Assistance Center (LAC) offers skills-based tutoring across a variety of disciplines, including English. Appointments are available on a weekly or one-time basis. For weekly tutoring, you'll need a referral from your instructor; sign-ups usually begin a couple of weeks into the semester. For a one-time tutoring session, fill out the intake form on the LAC website and bring it with you the first time you visit. You may even be able to make an appointment for the same day.

Campus Academic Resource Program (CARP)	Senior Program Coordinator: Morris Head	(415) 405-0971 carp1@sfsu.edu https://www.sfsu.edu/~carp1/	HSS 346

The Campus Academic Resource Program (CARP) offers both one-on-one and group tutoring, as well as workshops and support sessions, in a variety of subject areas. CARP even offers tutoring in the evening, unlike most other tutoring centers. Make an appointment by visiting or calling the CARP office; you cannot make CARP appointments via e-mail. Drop-in appointments are available on a first-come, first-serve basis, and are limited by tutor availability. Weekly tutoring is available; ask your instructor to refer you.

Educational Opportunity Program (EOP)

Phone: (415) 338-1085 Phone: (415) 338-1646 E-mail: eop@sfsu.edu	Student Services 201 Website: https://www.sfsu.edu/~eop/

Figuring out how to navigate college can be tough, and it can be even tougher if you're part of the first generation in your family to attend. The Educational Opportunity Program at SFSU is designed to help first-generation low-income college students succeed. (Most readers of this handbook are admitted freshmen, but if you are a high school student applying to SFSU, check the EOP website for eligibility requirements—students must apply to EOP at the same time they apply to the university.)

EOP is a comprehensive support system for students, providing outreach, tutoring, advising, and other support services, all under one umbrella. EOP programs include:

- Summer Bridge, a five-week program designed to help students transition from high school to the university. Students participating in Summer Bridge can earn up to six elective units.

- The Guardian Scholars Program, serving former foster-care youth

- Student Support Services, a program which provides intensive academic support to students for their first two years in college.

Metro Academies

Metro Academy of Health	Phone: (415) 338-3034 Email: metro@sfsu.edu	HSS 301 Website: https://metrohealth.sfsu.edu
Metro Early Childhood Academy	Phone: (415) 405-0737 Email: metroece@sfsu.edu	HSS 300 Website: https://metroece.sfsu.edu

Each Metro Academy is a "school within a school" that supports students through the first two years of college. The academies help students form learning communities, in which they take many classes as a cohort, including second-year composition, and are supported with tutoring and extra academic counseling.

The Metro Academy of Health serves students who are pursuing majors in health, but also many of the social sciences, such as political science and criminal justice. The Metro Early Childhood Academy serves students who are interested in early childhood education and social justice.

Incoming first-year students can apply to a Metro Academy for the fall or spring semester of their freshman year. Applications are reviewed on an ongoing basis, but if you are interested in applying to a Metro Academy, it's best to apply as early as possible for the best chance at securing one of the limited spaces; each academy serves about 140 students per year.

Each Metro Academy is a "school within a school" which supports students through the first two years of college.

The J. Paul Leonard Library

The campus library is one of the most important resources available to you as a student. Luckily for you, it's also a beautiful place to visit. The newly rebuilt J. Paul Leonard Library opened in the spring of 2012, and features a cafe, numerous study spaces, computer labs, printing services, a bookshop, digital media studios, and the Sutro Library, which is part of the California State Library and houses US local history, a rare book and manuscript collection, and an extensive genealogical collection.

For more information about library services and research tools, see the sections in Chapter 8 on the J. Paul Leonard Library website and Computer Labs and Study Spaces.

Undergraduate Advising Center

| Phone: (415) 338-2103 | Administration Building 211 |
| Email: advising@sfsu.edu | Website: https://www.sfsu.edu/~advising/ |

The Undergraduate Advising Center is a key resource for students. Whether or not your major has a mandatory advising policy (check the advising website to see if yours does), the Advising Center can help you make sure that you are on track to meet your major and graduation requirements.

In addition to traditional advising appointments, the Advising Center offers workshops, drop-in advising sessions, quick-question advising sessions, and an online advising module.

. . . the Advising Center can help you make sure that you are on track to meet your major and graduation requirements.

7

Policies and Procedures

Registration: Add/Drop Deadlines

Withdrawals

Important Dates and Deadlines

Attendance

Use of Electronic Devices/Cell Phones

Academic Honesty

Grades

SFSU Policy on Observance of Religious Holidays

SFSU Policy on Non-Discrimination

Campus Emergencies

During New Student Orientation, you will get helpful information about your FYC course, as well as about how to approach your first year as a college student at SFSU. One important element of success as a first-year college student is the ability to plan ahead, and knowing the important dates and deadlines, as well as the registration and add/drop deadlines, will allow you to do this. This chapter contains information about other important policies and procedures as well.

Registration: Add/Drop Deadlines

Use the following tables as a resource as you plan your first year and remember you can always get additional information through the SFSU Registrar's Office website.

Add Deadlines	
Orientation/ Priority Registration	During your assigned orientation, or Priority Registration Time, you will enroll in your chosen FYC course. (See Chapters 2 and 3 for more information about how you will make this selection.)
Weeks 1–3	This first week you should also receive confirmation of your enrollment through an e-mail sent to your SFSU account.
	Instructors may drop students who are absent on the first day of instruction, so we strongly recommend that you contact your instructor if you miss the first day, but still want to be enrolled in the class. Missing the first day doesn't **automatically** drop you from the course, but since it can happen at the instructor's discretion, you should make every effort to get in contact if an emergency prevents you from attending the first day.
	If for some reason you did not add an FYC Course during orientation or your Early/Final Priority Appointment Time, you can register with a permit number from an instructor who has an available seat in her class. All your holds must be cleared and your fees paid.
Week 4–End of Semester	Course additions are not permitted.

Drop Deadlines	
Weeks 1–2	You can drop courses without obtaining approval from anyone, but we strongly recommend speaking with an academic advisor before dropping a course.
Weeks 3–15	During this time, you can only withdraw from a class for **serious and compelling reasons**, and will need to petition using a **Withdrawal Petition**. Individual withdrawals will need to be approved by the instructor, chair, and dean and may likely require **documentation** (like a doctor's note). If your petition is approved, you will receive a "W" on your record.

While knowing deadlines is important, it's also helpful as a student to know the appropriate etiquette for adding and dropping a college course. Here are some tips to guide you should you find yourself looking to add or drop a course:

- Check open enrollments: don't just show up to a class. Look online to see which classes have open seats. You can for open FYC courses through the Composition Office Hotline at (415) 338-2128.

- E-mail the instructor directly. Introduce yourself and inquire politely about the possibility of adding the course or being put on the instructor's wait-list. (Even in courses without official wait lists, the instructor may be keeping an unofficial list of students who have requested add codes.) You can save yourself time this way and make a positive first impression.

- If you are dropping a course in favor of another one, make sure you drop first before adding the new one.

- If you are enrolled in a year-long FYC course, remember that you cannot switch classes between semesters. You are required to take English 105 from the same instructor, and at the same day/time, as you took English 104.

Withdrawals

Students sometimes also have questions about the withdrawal process. Keep in mind that if you find yourself having to petition for a withdrawal, you will likely need to consult with your academic advisor, as well as possibly your instructor, and maybe the chair or the dean. So that you have a sense of what would be considered by the university to be **serious or compelling reasons** to withdraw from a course, here are some examples:

- Serious and extended personal or family illness

- Personal or family crisis

- Significant financial problem making it impossible to come to class

- Change in work schedule making it impossible to come to class

- Change in child or other dependent care making it impossible to come to class

- Unanticipated and valuable educational or employment opportunity at the same time as class

- Military or extended jury service making it impossible to come to class

> *While knowing deadlines is important, it's also helpful as a student to know the appropriate etiquette for adding and dropping a college course.*

> *If you are enrolled in a year-long FYC course, remember that you cannot switch classes between semesters.*

So you can compare, the following would be considered **generally not acceptable reasons** for withdrawing by the University:

- Grades or academic standing

- Don't need or want the course

- Taking too many units

- Need to study for other courses

- Having problems with the instructor

- Will retake the course later

- Changed majors

Important Dates and Deadlines

Here is a summary of the important SFSU dates and deadlines for Fall 2013/ Spring 2014. Putting these dates, together with other important deadlines in your FYC classroom, into your online or physical calendar will help you be prepared for whatever the semester may bring you.

Fall 2013		
Monday	August 26	First Day of Instruction
Monday	September 2	Labor Day—No Classes
Monday	September 9	Drop Deadline
Monday	November 11	Veterans Day—No Classes
Mon–Sat	November 25–30	Fall Recess—No Classes
Saturday	December 14	Final Exams
Monday	December 16	Last Day of Classes
Tue–Sat	December 17–21	Final Exams

Spring 2014		
Monday	January 27	First Day of Instruction
Friday	February 7	Drop Deadline
Mon–Sat	March 24–29	Spring Recess
Monday	March 31	Cesar Chavez Day—No Classes
Friday	May 16	Last Day of Classes
Sat–Fri	May 17–23	Final Exams

Attendance

In your FYC course, attendance is important to your success, as everything you will do in class is directly related to your development as a writer. Because of this, you can expect your instructor to keep track of your absences, and you should track them carefully as well. You are expected to be present in class every day your class is scheduled, and you can expect your instructor to be present as well. Should your instructor be required to miss a class, a notice will be posted at your classroom, and you may also be contacted through e-mail with specific instructions (see Chapter 6 for more details on what to expect in the event of a class cancellation).

Your instructor will inform you of her specific attendance and lateness policy, but please note that because we believe attendance is so vital to your success in class, missing more than **one week of class** may affect your grade, and missing more than **two weeks** may result in you failing or being dropped from the course.

If you cannot make a particular class, it is a good idea to contact your instructor, but please note that this does not "excuse" your absence. You may also need to get in touch with a classmate to get copies of class notes, assignments, or any other materials from him or her. Even if you are absent, you are still responsible for all class work and homework and for meeting assignment deadlines.

Use of Electronic Devices/Cell Phones

Please note that these policies are made with the idea that you are in college to gain knowledge from the classes you've signed up for, and ultimately, a degree in your chosen field that you will have for life. To accomplish this, you need to be not just physically present, but also mentally present, which means not using technology to be "elsewhere" in any way during class. Appropriate and inappropriate uses of technology in the first year composition classroom are outlined below.

■ *Cell Phones*

Cell phones and other electronic devices such as iPods and mp3 players must be silenced during instruction. When you sit down for class, remove your earbuds or headphones, and put your phone away. At no point during class is it appropriate to be texting—and yes, your instructor can see you when you are texting under the desk. Going out in the hallway to answer or take a call is also unacceptable during class time.

In your FYC course, attendance is important to your success, as everything you will do in class is directly related to your development as a writer.

. . . you need to be not just physically present, but also mentally present . . .

At no point during class is it appropriate to be texting—and yes, your instructor can see you when you are texting under the desk.

■ *Laptops and Smartphones*

Laptops, tablets, and smartphones are welcome in the classroom as educational tools to enhance instruction. Here are some ways laptops (or in some cases smartphones) may be used appropriately during class:

- Accessing online required texts or textbooks

- Accessing class websites, such as iLearn

- Researching content for an essay

- Taking notes

- Writing drafts

For no reason should you be using your electronic devices to surf social media sites, play computer games, answer e-mail, or work on homework for another class. Your instructor will advise you of the penalty for utilizing technology inappropriately in class.

Academic Honesty

In FYC courses, we place emphasis on the process of integrating your own ideas with those of others in writing. Using sources appropriately and effectively is, you will recall, one of the goals of FYC, and these are skills your instructor will help you build. In the context of this dialogue—between your ideas and the ideas of others—we take academic honesty and integrity very seriously.

Plagiarism is a form of cheating or fraud, and students who plagiarize can be expelled from the university.

Part of this learning process is making sure that you, the student, understand what plagiarism is and how to avoid it by properly assigning credit in all your class work. Plagiarism is a form of cheating or fraud, and students who plagiarize can be expelled from the university. The English Department has a number of procedures and guidelines for reporting plagiarism, including the following definition:

> Plagiarism is a form of cheating or fraud; it occurs when a student misrepresents the work of another as his or her own. Plagiarism may consist of using the ideas, sentences, paragraphs, or the whole text of another without appropriate acknowledgment, but it also includes employing or allowing another person to write or substantially alter a work that a student then submits as his or her own.

Here are some examples of acts of plagiarism and academic dishonesty:

- Purchasing, borrowing, or stealing an essay, whether online, from a friend, from a family member, or a tutor, or from a database

- Having someone else write, revise, or edit your work

- Selling, loaning, or giving your work to someone else to copy from or to pass of as their own work

- Faking citations, statistics, or quotes

- Using an essay from a "paper mill" in whole or in part

- Copying and pasting text from sources without proper citation

- Translating a foreign language article

- Any act of obvious academic dishonesty

On the first day of class your instructor will provide you with a syllabus that will include a full definition of plagiarism as well as the penalties for plagiarizing. Your instructor may also use specific anti-plagiarism software (see the section on Turnitin in Chapter 8). If this is the case, she will give you more information during class about how you will be using the technology, as well as additional help if you need it.

All instances of plagiarism in FYC classrooms will be reported to the Dean of the College and may be reported to the University Judicial Affairs Officer for further action. Repeated acts of plagiarism will result in your being disenrolled from the university.

Keep in mind that throughout the course itself you will receive instruction on how to properly cite sources and how to avoid plagiarizing the work of others. Your instructor understands that learning how to incorporate sources effectively is a challenging process. As you are learning, it's possible you may make mistakes, and may need to revise your work, or meet with your instructor for clarification; this will be determined between you and your instructor.

When you are in doubt about whether or how to incorporate the words and ideas of others into your own text, the best thing you can do is ask your instructor.

Keep in mind that throughout the course itself you will receive instruction on how to properly cite sources and how to avoid plagiarizing the work of others.

Grades

As you learned in Chapter 1, grading in FYC courses is A, B, C, or NC. Your instructor will provide you with a detailed description of his grading policies, and you will be provided with a course syllabus that will describe how your final course grade will be calculated. Throughout the course, you will receive written feedback on your writing that will help you revise and better your work. You should always have a sense of how you're doing grade-wise in the class through this feedback.

Your instructor will provide you with a detailed description of his grading policies . . .

If you have any questions about grading policies, you should feel free to discuss this with your instructor at an appropriate time, like during a scheduled office hour appointment. In Chapter 4, the section on "How to Succeed in FYC" and in Chapter 6, the section on "Office Hour Etiquette" provide you with helpful tips for how to navigate office hour appointments, so peruse these sections for additional support.

The following set of definitions of possible semester grades in first-year composition courses is taken from the 2012–2013 SFSU Bulletin:

■ *Basic Definitions*

The following symbols shall be used in evaluating student performance. Performance will be interpreted to reflect the quality of the student's accomplishment relative to the standards set for each course.

A: Performance of the student has been of the highest level, showing sustained excellence in meeting course responsibilities.

B: Performance of the student has been good, though not of the highest level.

C: Performance of the student has been adequate, satisfactorily meeting the course requirements.

NC: (No Credit) Performance of the student has been less than that of CR level.

W: (Withdrawal) Indicates that the student was permitted to withdraw from the course after the 4th week of instruction with the approval of the instructor and appropriate campus officials. It carries no connotation of quality of student performance and is not used in calculating grade point average or progress points. Remember that the process of withdrawing from a course is a students' responsibility, and must be approved by the instructor, chair, and dean. The student may also need to supply evidence of a serious or compelling reason for withdrawing from the course. At the start of this chapter, some examples of acceptable reasons for withdrawing are listed for your clarification.

■ *Keeping Track of Your Grades*

At the end of the semester, you can access your final grade through MySFSU . . .

At the end of the semester, you can access your final grade through MySFSU, but you should have a sense of how you're doing in the course throughout the semester through the written feedback and grades assigned on your class work. In addition, your instructor might provide you with access to a gradebook through a course website, like iLearn, or you may have a progress report conference midway through the semester.

Keep in mind, as pointed out in Chapter 8, different instructors use online gradebooks in different ways, so don't be afraid to ask for clarification about this from your instructor if you are unsure. Regardless, you should always keep your graded essays, papers, quizzes, and assignments so you have a personal record of your status in the class.

■ *Course Repeat Policy*

Students can only repeat a class once. If you take English 114, for example, and receive a Withdrawal (W) or No Credit (NC), you can only take the class one more time at SFSU. This policy applies to all undergraduate classes at SFSU, not just required English classes. If you are repeating English 114 or another course and believe you may not pass or need to withdraw from the course, make plans to see an advisor immediately.

■ *Grading Disputes*

In the event that you think you have received an unfair or incorrect grade, you should always attempt to first discuss the situation with your instructor. Often, a face-to-face meeting will help clarify an instructor's evaluation of your coursework. This is another reason why it is important to keep your graded work as it is passed back to you. In rare cases, a scoring error may have occurred, which your instructor will be happy to correct, or your instructor can explain in better detail her reasons for assigning you the grade you received.

Often, a face-to-face meeting will help clarify an instructor's evaluation of your coursework.

In the event that you are unable to resolve a dispute with your instructor, you should contact the appropriate Program Coordinator for your course, listed below:

- ENG 104,105, and 114 courses: Tara Lockhart, taralock@sfsu.edu

- Other composition classes: Sugie Goen-Salter, sgoen@sfsu.edu

- CMS classes: Lisa Heyer, lheyer@sfsu.edu

■ *Grade Changes*

For the most part, the grade you receive at the end of your course is the grade you will keep, except in very rare cases—for example, cases of administrative or instructor error. Here are a few specific guidelines about the rare grade change:

- Letter grades are not convertible to other letter grades and NC grades are not convertible to CR grades except in cases of instructor or administrative error. All grade changes are by petition and require a recommendation of a grade change by the instructor and the approval of the department chair and/or college dean.

■ Except in cases of instructor or administrative error, CR/NC grades are not convertible to letter grades or vice versa. All grade change requests involving the CR/NC option are also by petition, with a recommendation by the instructor and the approval of the department chair and/or college dean. Requests for reasons other than clerical error are subject to review by the Board of Appeals and Review.

■ A student wishing to request a retroactive grade change, withdrawal, or addition must initiate the request during the semester in attendance immediately following the semester when the original grade was assigned or the course in question was offered.

■ *Student Appeal for a Grade Change*

In the unlikely event that you do find yourself petitioning for a grade change, here is some information about the process, which we've taken from the 2012–2013 SFSU Bulletin:

San Francisco State University policy, consistent with California State University policy, guarantees the student a right to appeal a final course grade when the student believes that the assigned grade does not reflect what the student has earned according to the criteria for grading as outlined by the instructor of the course. SF State policy states that: (1) It is the responsibility of the instructor of each course to define his/her grading policy and criteria as early in the semester and as explicitly as possible while conforming to accepted university practices. If there is any deviation from this original statement of course policy, all affected students should be informed. (2) It shall be assumed that the grade assigned is correct and that the student appealing the grade must justify the need for a change of the grade assigned. (3) Normally, grade appeals should be resolved informally between the student and faculty involved. (4) A student who believes s/he has been assigned an improper grade should meet with the instructor of record and together review the grading procedures used to determine the grade assigned on the student's transcript. If, after careful review of the grading procedures, the student is still dissatisfied, or if the instructor of record refuses to take part in the informal process, the student may initiate the formal grade appeal procedure.

SFSU Policy on Observance of Religious Holidays

At San Francisco State University, and in the FYC classroom, we seek to respect and accommodate students wishing to observe religious holidays when such observances require students to be absent from class activities. Keep in mind, though, that it is your responsibility as a student to inform your instructors, in writing, about such holidays during the first two weeks of the class each semester. If such holidays occur during the first two weeks of the semester, you must notify your instructors, in writing, at least three days before the date that you will be absent.

It is the responsibility of the instructor to make every reasonable effort to honor the student request without penalty, and of the student to make up the work missed. You will probably find this policy in your instructor's syllabus, and he will be aware of the religious holiday calendar, but remember it is the student's responsibility to provide a written request if you wish to be excused from class for religious observation.

SFSU Policy on Non-Discrimination

Just as we wish to accommodate your observance of religious holidays, we also seek at San Francisco State, and in the FYC classroom, to provide you with a safe environment in which to learn and participate with comfort. Discrimination is not tolerated for any reason on campus. The following information on our Non-Discrimination Policy is taken from the 2012–2013 SFSU Bulletin:

. . . we also seek at San Francisco State, and in the FYC classroom, to provide you with a safe environment in which to learn and participate with comfort.

■ *Race, Color, Ethnicity, National Origin, Age, and Religion*

The California State University does not discriminate on the basis of race, color, ethnicity, national origin, age, or religion in its programs and activities, including admission and access. Federal and state laws prohibit such discrimination. The Office of University Counsel has been designated to coordinate the efforts of San Francisco State University to comply with all applicable federal and state laws prohibiting discrimination on these bases. Inquiries concerning compliance may be presented to the Office of University Counsel at (415) 338-2998.

■ *Disability*

The California State University does not discriminate on the basis of disability in its programs and activities, including admission and access. Federal and state laws prohibit such discrimination. The Disability Programs and Resource Center director has been designated to coordinate the efforts of San Francisco State University to comply with all applicable federal and state laws prohibiting discrimination on the basis of disability. Call (415) 338-2472 (voice/TTY) for inquiries regarding compliance.

■ *Sex/Gender/Gender Identity/Sexual Orientation*

The California State University does not discriminate on the basis of sex, gender, gender identity, or sexual orientation in its programs and activities, including admission and access. Federal and state laws prohibit such discrimination. The Office of University Counsel has been designated to coordinate the efforts of San Francisco State University to comply with all applicable federal and state laws prohibiting discrimination on these bases. Call (415) 338-2998 for inquiries regarding compliance.

The California State University is committed to providing equal opportunities to male and female CSU students in all campus programs, including intercollegiate athletics.

■ *HIV/AIDS Policy*

Students and employees with HIV/AIDS shall be afforded unrestricted classroom attendance, working conditions, use of university facilities, and participation in cocurricular and extracurricular activities as long as they are physically and psychologically able to do so.

For more information, individuals are encouraged to contact Student Health Services, members of the AIDS Coordinating Committee at (415) 338-7339, Human Resources Department, Office of Faculty Affairs, or the Dean of Students office.

■ *Inquiries Concerning Compliance*

Inquiries concerning compliance or the application of these laws to programs and activities of San Francisco State University may be referred to the specific campus officer(s) identified above or to the Regional Director of the Office for Civil Rights, United States Department of Education, 50 Beale Street, Suite 7200, San Francisco, California 94105.

Campus Emergencies

University Police Department
Emergency: (415) 338-2222 or 911
Non-Emergency and Campus Escort: (415) 338-7200
Anonymous Crime Tip Line: (415) 338-3030
Email: upd@sfsu.edu

University Police Department, North State Drive
Website: http://www.sfsu.edu/~upd

Traditionally, San Francisco State has a long history as a peaceful campus. However, as a student it's important for you to know what to do in case of an emergency on campus, as well as how you will be contacted should an emergency occur.

In the event of an emergency, do not hesitate to dial 911. When you dial 911 from a campus phone, your call will be routed directly to the University Police Department. When calling 911 from a mobile phone, tell the dispatcher that you are on campus, ask to be routed to the University Police Department, and give your location as accurately as possible—include the building name and room number, if you can.

A comprehensive list of campus emergency services and programs—as well as crime statistics, emergency preparedness recommendations, and safety tips—can be found at the University Police Department website, but we've highlighted some key recommendations and programs below.

■ *In Case of Emergency*

In the event of an emergency, do not hesitate to dial 911. Emergency phones are spread throughout the campus and on every level of the main parking garage; they are clearly marked. Yellow courtesy phones, which can be used to dial any campus extension, are also spread throughout the campus. You may also use these phones to dial 911 to connect to the University Police Department. The University Police Department also offers the following tips for dealing with emergencies:

- Call 911 and/or locate and pull the nearest fire alarm.

- Evacuate the building for all alarms.

- In an emergency, listen for direction from your instructor. Take action to keep yourselves and others safe.

- It may be some time before you are allowed to re-enter the building, so if you are not in immediate danger, take a moment to collect your belongings.

- Remain calm, and evacuate the building in an orderly fashion.

- You may be called upon to assist others. **Be prepared to do your part.** Help others to evacuate the building in an orderly fashion. If someone is injured or disabled and not able to leave the building, note their location and immediately contact emergency personnel.

In the event of an emergency, do not hesitate to dial 911.

Yellow courtesy phones, which can be used to dial any campus extension, are also spread throughout the campus.

- Once you have left the building, move a safe distance away and stay in one place.

- Do not re-enter the building until emergency service personnel have announced that it is safe to do so.

■ *Campus Alliance for a Risk-Free Environment (CARE)*

Members of the CARE team are available to escort you to or from your vehicle, classroom, or campus apartment. Team members work under the supervision of the University Police Department and carry two-way radios to maintain direct contact with the police department. You can identify CARE team members by their distinctive red polo shirts or jackets with CARE written in white lettering down the back.

Requesting an Escort

If you would like a campus escort, use a campus yellow courtesy phone or call the University Police Department non-emergency line at (415) 338-7200 and let them know where you would like to be met. A CARE member will arrive in about 10–15 minutes to escort you.

Nighttime Shuttle

Nighttime on-campus transportation is available to all students with temporary or permanent disabilities. This service is available Monday through Saturday from 4:30–11:00 p.m. Shuttle rides can be arranged in advance or requested by telephone as needed. To request a shuttle cart ride during the evening, call the University Police Department non-emergency line at (415) 338-7200. Students must be registered with the Disability Programs and Resource Center (DPRC) to make advance appointments for each semester. (See the Disability Programs and Resource Center section on page 97.)

■ *Campus Emergency Notification System*

One of the first things you should do as a first-time college student at SFSU is to take a moment to enroll in the campus Emergency Notification System to make sure you receive all emergency alerts. Log in to https://www.sfsu.edu/student and click on "Contact Information." The Emergency Notification system is designed to rapidly disseminate information and instructions in the event of an emergency by sending messages via phone, voicemail, TTY, text, and e-mail to members of the campus community.

Notification systems like this have become part and parcel of emergency preparedness strategies on college campuses across the country. While this notification system is an important part of the emergency preparedness plan for SFSU, we also encourage you to take advantage of preparedness training and review information available through the Office of Emergency Preparedness and the University Police Department.

Technology Used in FYC

iLearn

Phone: (415) 405-5555
E-mail: ilearn@sfsu.edu

LIB 220
Websites: https://ilearn.sfsu.edu
http://atcentral.sfsu.edu

Many instructors, including many first-year composition instructors, use iLearn, SFSU's course management system. Instructors often use their iLearn course websites to post readings, assignments, and handouts, which you'll be expected to download and print. (For information on campus computer and print labs, see the section on computer labs and study spaces on page 86.) You might also be asked to turn in assignments electronically to iLearn, to participate in a discussion forum, to help create a wiki, and more.

Because iLearn sites are customizable, different instructors use iLearn in different ways . . .

Because iLearn sites are customizable, different instructors use iLearn in different ways, so you may encounter different features on different course iLearn sites, or even the same feature used in different ways. If you have questions, be sure to ask your instructor or contact iLearn help by using the handy links on the login page. If your instructor has included the iLearn help links on your course page, you can even contact iLearn help directly from your course website.

Once you've logged in to iLearn, you'll see a list of your courses in the left-hand sidebar. If one of the classes you're enrolled in is not listed, this means that the course is not open to students, either because the instructor does not plan to use iLearn at all, or the instructor has not yet made the site visible to students. To visit your course page, just click on the course name.

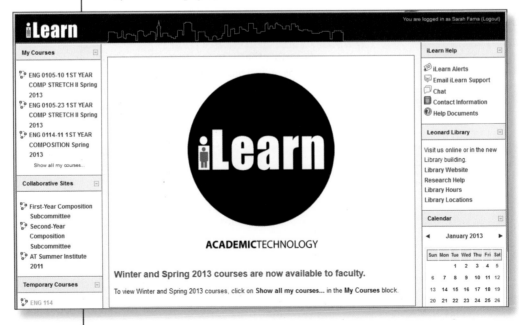

■ *Browser Compatibility Recommendations*

The Academic Technology department at SFSU, which develops and maintains iLearn services, recommends that you use Mozilla Firefox as your internet browser when you are working with iLearn, because this is the browser on which iLearn features are most commonly tested. For more info on compatibility requirements, visit http://atcentral.sfsu.edu. To find info on using iLearn features, check out the support documents and tutorials at http://at.sfsu.edu. Remember, iLearn is a constant work in progress, so features and tutorials are subject to change.

> *. . . use Mozilla Firefox as your internet browser when you are working with iLearn . . .*

■ *Course Page*

Many instructors use the top of the iLearn page to provide useful information relevant to the course, such as the instructor's contact information and office hours, a link to the syllabus, or a description of the course and its goals. Every course also includes a News forum (see below), which your instructor may use to keep you informed of happenings in or relating to the course.

Course navigation □

ENG114TEMP-SP13

▸ Participants

▸ Reports

▸ Section 0

▸ Section 1

▸ Section 2

▸ Section 3

▸ Section 4

As you scroll down, you'll see a series of boxes; instructors may use these to organize information for their courses, either according to type or chronologically. For example, some instructors use each section to outline each week of the course, or each class meeting; often, these instructors will also include a sidebar widget that allows you to skip to the current section, rather than scrolling through the entire page. Instructors use these sections in a variety of ways, so be sure to spend some time at the beginning of the semester exploring the iLearn page of each course you're enrolled in, so that you know where to find everything.

■ *Assignments*

Many instructors will ask you to turn in at least some assignments electronically. Ask your instructor which file format (Word documents, PDFs, etc.) she prefers you to use—you don't want to turn in an assignment that your instructor can't open or read.

Homework Assignment

NOTE

Be sure to check your assignment sheets, or the instructions provided on iLearn by your instructor, for due dates. Don't rely on the "Due date" named on the assignment link, as it's possible that your instructor simply did not bother changing the default end date provided by iLearn when he created the assignment link. When in doubt, double-check with your instructor.

■ *Gradebook*

Not all instructors use the built-in iLearn gradebook, and those who do may use it in very different ways. For example, some instructors might use iLearn only to record the grades students receive on formal writing assignments. In that case, the student's "grade" on iLearn would be inaccurate because other key grades—like homework and participation grades, for example—aren't included on iLearn.

Other instructors might use iLearn to record formal writing assignment grades, informal writing assignment grades, and information on student attendance, but don't set up their iLearn gradebook to reflect the way assignments are going to be weighted in accordance with the course syllabus. In that case, the student's grade on iLearn would be inaccurate because iLearn is using its default method of grade calculation, instead of the method the instructor will be using to calculate the student's course grade.

If you want an estimate of your grade in the course, the best thing to do is to stop by your instructor's office during office hours, or write your instructor an e-mail, and ask how you're doing. Alternatively, you can always estimate your own grade by using the information in the syllabus (which tells you how much each type of assignment is worth) and the scores you've received on various assignments to calculate your approximate course grade.

NOTE

One of the iLearn features that many students find confusing is the gradebook. Long story short—the grade you see in your iLearn gradebook may be very different from your actual grade in the class! Unless your instructor has specifically stated that the iLearn gradebook accurately reflects students' grades in the course, do not assume the "course grade" shown on iLearn is a reflection of your actual grade in the course.

■ *Forums*

Class discussions are a great way to explore issues, ideas, and arguments—but we don't always have as much time for in-class discussion as we'd like. The Forums feature on iLearn allows a whole class or small groups to bring those discussions online.

❖ Introductions forum

Although forum discussions are asynchronous (everyone isn't necessarily discussing at the same time; each participant is popping in and out to post when it's convenient for them), they can still be rich and productive discussions. There are a few different types of iLearn forums.

News forum

Every course has a news forum, which your instructor may use to post information relevant to the course. The default setting is for everyone enrolled in the class to be "subscribed" to the forum—that is, for everyone to automatically receive notifications about updates to the forum via e-mail.

Even if your instructor has set the forum up so that subscribing is optional, it's a good idea to subscribe—that way, you'll know right away when news has been posted. (To make sure you receive updates promptly, see the section on setting up your SFSU e-mail account below.) If you notice you aren't receiving your forum digest e-mails, check your spam folder, and make sure to adjust your spam settings so that you receive e-mails generated by iLearn.

Single simple discussion

This type of forum is the most straightforward; everyone posts in the same thread, which focuses on one discussion topic. Replies are indented to show who replied to whom.

Standard forum for general use

This type of forum (along with the very similar "blog-like" format described below) is one of the most flexible. In a standard forum for general use, each participant can start a new discussion thread, or more than one discussion thread, which others can then respond to.

Blog-like format

This is a new type of forum, which debuted in the spring of 2013. Conceptually, this type of forum is very similar to the standard forum for general use, but it's formatted to show the discussion threads more clearly before you click into them.

Each person posts one discussion

In this type of forum, each participant can initiate his or her own discussion—but can create only *one* new discussion thread.

Q&A

Sometimes, your instructor wants you to consider your own response to a discussion question or topic carefully, before you encounter your peers' responses. A Q&A forum helps you do this. In this type of forum, your instructor will post a question or discussion topic to begin the thread. Participants cannot see other participants' replies to a discussion topic until they have posted their own answer or response. After that, participants can respond to each other, as in a single simple discussion.

> **Sometimes, your instructor wants you to consider your own response to a discussion question or topic carefully, before you encounter your peers' responses.**

NOTE

Just as in an in-class discussion, be respectful and professional in online class discussions. Keep in mind that it's a lot harder to convey tone in writing than in a face-to-face discussion, and choose your words carefully. Likewise, it's a good idea to read your comment out loud, check for potentially confusing ambiguities, and proofread before you hit "post"—do your best to make sure that others can actually read and understand your post as you intended it to be understood.

■ *Other iLearn Discussion Tools*

In addition to forums, which are the most commonly used discussion feature on iLearn, your instructor might also choose to use some of the other iLearn tools that enable discussion and collaboration.

Wikis

You are likely familiar with the concept of a wiki thanks to Wikipedia, the online encyclopedia. Wikis allow many people to work together to write and edit a text. iLearn has a wiki feature, and your instructor may use this feature to give the entire class, or small groups of students, the opportunity to collaborate on a text. Each participant in a wiki can add to or edit the document.

Like forums, wiki collaborations are asynchronous, with participants working on the document individually at different times, rather than everyone working at the same time. In fact, only one participant can be editing a wiki at any one time, so this feature **can't** be used for simultaneous discussion.

Blackboard Collaborate

Sometimes you want to work together with a group of people all at the same time, to discuss or collaborate, but it's not possible to meet in the same physical space. Since a single class may include students commuting from San Jose to Oakland to Petaluma, which is not an uncommon problem for students at SFSU. Luckily, iLearn includes a useful collaboration and web conferencing tool called Blackboard Collaborate, which allows students to work together on a virtual whiteboard, chat, and even videoconference.

Chat

Your instructor can set up iLearn Chat sessions so that you and your classmates can participate in real-time discussions as a class or in small groups.

■ eReserves

University libraries have long had "reserved book rooms," where instructors set aside books for students from their courses. The library eReserves are simply a digital extension of that concept; your instructor and the library work together to make a PDF file of the text accessible to you while adhering to the "fair use" provisions of copyright law. Now, these course eReserves are integrated directly into the course iLearn page.

If your instructor has readings on eReserves for you, you'll see a block labeled "E-Reserves" in one of the sidebars. You can click on the "View eReserves" button to see the list of PDFs your instructor has made available to you. Your instructor may also link directly to these documents in iLearn sections.

■ Library Resource links

If your instructor assigns readings which are available in one of the library databases, he may link to it as a library resource. Unlike eReserve documents, you can't open a library resource PDF directly from the iLearn link; you'll have to click through to the library database where the file is actually stored and download the PDF (or read the document in another format) from there.

This process can be a little confusing the first few times. Because you're trying to access material from a library database, you'll need to have a library PIN set

iLearn includes a useful collaboration and web conferencing tool called Blackboard Collaborate, which allows students to work together on a virtual whiteboard, chat, and even videoconference.

If your instructor assigns readings which are available in one of the library databases, he may link to it as a library resource.

up first; think of it as your virtual library card. Incidentally, you don't need to use your PIN and log in if you are accessing a library database from a campus computer classroom—the library databases "know" that users of those computers are students, and allow access automatically.

■ *Web resources*

Your instructor may integrate links to outside web resources into your course iLearn page. These might be readings, useful campus resources and websites, other academic resources, or online assignments. (See "Other Technologies" below.)

■ *Turnitin*

When you become a college student, you become part of the community of academic writers. Your credibility as a member of this community depends in large part on your being meticulous about giving credit when you use the words and ideas of others in your own writing. The way we cite sources—the way we give credit—varies from discipline to discipline and from one writing situation to the next, so we recognize that citing sources properly can be a tricky process for students in the early stages of their college career.

> Turnitin Assignment ✎ → ✛ ✎ ×2 ✗ ⊛ ▮▮

We don't expect you to be an expert by the time you leave your FYC class, let alone when you enter it. A key goal of FYC is to give you tools that help you figure out when and how to cite, and one of the tools your instructor may choose to use is Turnitin.

You might be familiar with Turnitin from high school, but many FYC instructors use it a little differently—offering it as a revision tool to students during the essay drafting process, rather than just using it to "catch" plagiarism after assignments have been turned in. Because its "plagiarism-detection" software compares your writing to millions of other texts in its database and highlights matches, Turnitin allows you to see some potential problems with your use of sources and address those problems when you revise, learning better citation practices in the process.

■ *Quizzes*

Your instructor can create and administer quizzes right from the course iLearn site. Although first-year composition instructors don't create and administer quizzes as frequently as instructors in some other courses and disciplines, your

---

When you become a college student, you become part of the community of academic writers.

You might be familiar with Turnitin from high school, but many FYC instructors use it a little differently . . .

instructor might use this feature to check in with a class to make sure that everyone is grasping a key concept. Quizzes on iLearn can vary widely in terms of content and structure; this tool allows instructors to employ many different question types, including multiple-choice, true/false, short answer, and essay questions, among others.

☑ Quiz #1 ✎ ➜ ✛ ✂ ×2 ✖ 👁 🔒

Some quizzes are only "open" for a specified length of time, so make sure you know the deadline for submitting all of your answers. Because the quiz feature can be used so many different ways, and each instructor has so much flexibility in how he can design an iLearn quiz, we won't go into further detail here; your instructor will explain what he expects you to do.

NOTE

When you are done answering the questions and have reviewed your work (if permitted to do so) make sure you click the "Submit all and finish" button on the last page—otherwise your answers will not be saved when the quiz ends.

■ *Choice*

Choice is a feature which allows your instructor to ask a single question and poll student responses.

■ *Lesson*

The Lesson activity module allows your instructor to create content pages or activities; these may be used to introduce and explore a new concept, review material already covered in the class, or as scenario or decision-making exercises.

■ *CourseStream*

Although few first-year composition instructors use this feature on a regular basis, CourseStream allows your instructor to record a lecture or screencapture and post the video to iLearn. Some instructors use this feature to post entire lectures, though this is rarely done in first-year composition courses. In first-year composition, instructors who use this technology generally do so to post simple tutorials on how to use a software or web tool, though a few also use it to give students feedback on writing assignments by recording a screencapture of the assignment and their verbal feedback.

SFSU E-mail

Division of Information Technology Website: http://doit.sfsu.edu	SFSU Login: http://www.sfsu.edu/login.htm	Help Desk Website: helpdesk@sfsu.edu Phone: (415) 338-1420

Every student is assigned an SFSU e-mail address. This e-mail address is the primary means your instructors have for getting in touch with you, because this SFSU address is the one used to create class distribution lists on your class rosters and iLearn Quickmail.

If you do not plan on using your SFSU e-mail as a primary e-mail, run to a computer right now and set up your account so that all mail sent to your SFSU e-mail will be forwarded to an e-mail address that you check on a regular basis . . .

If you do not plan on using your SFSU e-mail as a primary e-mail, run to a computer right now and set up your account so that all mail sent to your SFSU e-mail will be forwarded to an e-mail address that you check on a regular basis, because otherwise, you **will** miss important messages from your instructors. Here are the instructions for setting up forwarding on your account, as taken from the SFSU Division of Information Technology website:

1. Sign in at http://live.sfsu.edu.

2. From the mail view, select **Options > See All Options . . . .**

3. Select **Forward your email**.

4. Enter the address you want to forward your email to in the **Forward my email to:** field. It may be necessary to scroll down the page to see it.

5. Verify the **Keep a copy of forwarded messages in Outlook Web App** checkbox is **unchecked**.

6. Click on **Start Forwarding**.

7. To return from the Options page to the mail view click on **My Mail**.

8. Test by sending a message to your @mail.sfsu.edu address, then check and make sure it has forwarded correctly. Some mail services won't show the forwarded e-mail if it was sent from the same account it is forwarded to, so use a separate e-mail account for the test, or ask a friend to send the test message for you.

■ *E-mail Etiquette*

When writing an e-mail to a faculty or staff member, put your best face forward.

When writing an e-mail to a faculty or staff member, put your best face forward. Below are some e-mail etiquette basics:

- ■ Spell the recipient's name correctly.

- Include a clear subject line so that the recipient has an idea of what the message is about.

- Address the recipient appropriately: if you're writing to a professor, "Professor Smith" would be an appropriate form of address. "Ms. Smith" would not. If you're not sure, just say "Hello" and leave it at that.

- Remind your instructors which class and section you're in, and sign e-mails with your first and last name. That way, your instructors won't have to sit there figuring out which "Dave" is writing to them, or worse, who in the world "d_dawg@me.com" might be.

- Before sending an e-mail to your instructor with a question about the class or an assignment, consider where you might be able to find the information you need, and check the syllabus, assignment sheet, the iLearn site, and/or this handbook to see if your question has already been answered.

- Proofread carefully before you hit "send." If the recipient can't understand your message, then there really isn't much point in sending it.

Other Technologies

Not all instructors use the iLearn course management system; your instructor might have developed his or own course website on another platform, and many instructors incorporate other technologies into the classroom in a variety of ways. These may include, but are certainly not limited to:

Not all instructors use the iLearn course management system . . .

- Blogging platforms such as WordPress or Blogger

- Microbloging platforms such as Twitter or Tumblr

- Document sharing platforms such as Google Drive

- Appointment creation or signup websites such as Signup Genius

- Image sharing sites such as Flickr or Shutterfly

- Presentation software such as PowerPoint or Prezi

- Screencast technology such as Jing

Don't worry if you're unfamiliar with these technologies. Your instructor will explain how to use any applications you're using for class assignments.

NOTE

Always check to make sure the presentation software you're planning to use is compatible with the technology used in your classroom. If your instructor has not included these technical specifications on the assignment sheet, ask. You don't want to get up in front of the class to give your presentation, only to discover that the file won't open!

J. Paul Leonard Library Website

J. Paul Leonard Library	Research Assistance
Website: http://www.library.sfsu.edu	Call: (415) 338-1974
Phone: (415) 338-1974	Text: (415) 933-0385
E-mail: libweb@sfsu.edu	E-mail: libref@sfsu.edu

■ *Main Page*

The main page of the J. Paul Leonard Library website is designed to help you to quickly access library resources.

The main page of the J. Paul Leonard Library website is designed to help you to quickly access library resources. One thing we'd like to draw your particular attention to is the set of "Contact Us" links in the right hand sidebar. If you need help, you can contact the library via instant message (IM), text, phone, or e-mail, or by visiting the Research Assistance desk or scheduling a research consultation.

■ *Oasis Tutorial*

First-time freshmen are expected to complete the Basic Information Competence requirement by the end of their second semester, and the OASIS tutorial is the way that most students meet this requirement. The tutorial consists of eight chapters with quizzes, but you don't have to do it all in one sitting! This is a self-paced tutorial, and you are free to take the quizzes at your leisure, provided you complete the tutorial within one year of the date you first began OASIS, and by the end of your second semester as a freshman.

. . . complete the tutorial within one year of the date you first began OASIS, and by the end of your second semester as a freshman.

■ *Catalog*

To search the library catalogue, follow the "Library Catalog (books and more)" link from the main page. Use the library catalog to search the library's collection of books, articles, e-books, items in the library's hardcopy reserves, masters theses, music and scores, film and video, and special collections.

The catalog link takes you by default to the "Basic Search" field, where you can search by keyword, title, author, subject heading, or call number by entering terms in the search field. Or, you can choose to conduct a more advanced search by clicking the "Advanced Search" link, where you can fine-tune your search parameters much further.

The "Advanced Search" page offers a number of helpful search tips in a sidebar. If you need help, both search pages include a link to the library's IM service. Keep in mind that IM help is only available during the hours the Research Assistance desk is open—yet another very good reason you should give yourself plenty of time to work on your writing assignments, and not wait until 3:00 a.m. the night before.

■ *Databases*

One of the benefits of being a university student is the wealth of information at your fingertips. And we do mean "wealth"—academic journal subscriptions can cost tens or even hundreds of dollars per year, but the university library gives you access to thousands of academic journals for free. (Well, not exactly for free—your student fees help fund the library, after all.)

Although you can find recent issues of many journals in the library building, one of the easiest and most comprehensive ways to search for journal articles is to use the library's online databases. If you're unfamiliar with the concept, the important thing to know is that each database is a collection of millions of articles from thousands of different sources, which might include academic journals, newspapers, or magazines.

Databases often overlap in at least some regards, but each database is a little bit different in terms of the type of sources included within it: some databases (JSTOR, for example) are collections of primarily academic journals, while others (like LexisNexis) might focus just on news sources. When conducting research for class assignments, try using a variety of different databases to see which ones give you the most useful search results.

■ *Google Scholar*

If you like the ease and simplicity of Google, but want to find peer-reviewed academic journal articles instead of the usual result list full of questionable Wikipedia articles and insufferable blog posts, Google Scholar may be the search tool for you. To streamline your research process, click the Google Scholar link on the library homepage, log in with your student ID and pin number, then search the vast database of scholarly resources: you'll get your list of results in the familiar Google format, but with the added bonus of being able to click through to the article or resource itself in the library database (assuming the resource is part of our collection) via handy links in the sidebar.

If you need help, both search pages include a link to the library's IM service.

. . . you'll get your list of results in the familiar Google format, but with the added bonus of being able to click through to the article or resource itself in the library database

■ *Electronic Journals*

The Electronic Journals list is exactly what it sounds like: a list of scholarly journals which are available online through the library website. Use this link to search for specific journals by name or by subject to get access to that journal's digital archives.

■ *Link+*

One library can only hold so much, so most libraries are part of a larger system that facilitates inter-library loans. The SFSU library belongs to a larger network of libraries, and Link+ is the tool which allows you to search and borrow from other libraries within this network.

Computer Labs and Study Spaces

Computer labs on campus vary in terms of their policies, hours, amount of available assistance, and printing services. A comprehensive list of computer labs and their features and hours can be found at http://www.sfsu.edu/~doit/labs.htm.

One of the computer labs that is most accessible to you as a FYC student is the one in the English Tutoring Center (ETC) in HUM 290, which has 29 computers, all with internet access and a full suite of software applications. Visit the ETC computer lab website for up-to-date information on hours and policies: http://www.sfsu.edu/~etc/?q=node/2.

An additional computer lab in the Humanities building, in HUM 407, offers 16 computers, as well as printing services. Student assistants are available to provide you with help when using this lab. For hours, check the bulletin board outside the lab.

The computer lab in the library research commons is open 24 hours a day, except during some holidays—see the research commons website for exceptions and other policies: http://www.library.sfsu.edu/services/computers/infocommons.php.

One of the computer labs that is most accessible to you as a FYC student is the one in the English Tutoring Center (ETC) in HUM 290 . . .

NOTE

In addition to campus computer labs, there are also a number of computer classrooms on campus. These classrooms are NOT open computer labs. Check the sign outside the door if you're not sure, and don't walk into a class in progress and ask to use a computer—doing so is disruptive to the class in progress, and just plain rude.

The library building contains numerous study spaces on all floors of the library. You can find a directory of library study spaces by accessing the library floor map on the library website. Or, just visit the library and wander around—aside from the busiest times just before and during finals, you can usually find a quiet nook where you can focus on your work, or a comfy spot to meet with a study group. Also, groups can reserve a Group Study room on the first and ground floors of the library.

Although the Cesar Chavez student center may seem full of distractions (it's probably not a good idea to try to write an essay in the lower level Recreation and Dining area, with the temptations of air hockey and Ike's sandwiches right under your nose) the Rigoberta Menchu Hall on the Terrace level is a quiet space to read and relax.

Over in the Humanities building, you can find quiet, glass-enclosed study "pods" on the second, third, and fifth floors. Each study pod has been furnished with seating for about 20 students.

Of course, when the fog clears and the sun comes out (we promise, this does happen sometimes!) outdoor spaces like the Humanities courtyard, the outdoor seating in front of the campus cafes and student center, and the vast grassy quad in the center of campus all become lovely places to read or meet with a study group.

Also, groups can reserve a Group Study room on the first and ground floors of the library.

What Comes After FYC?

Your Second-Year Composition Requirement (2YC)

Your Final Writing Requirement: Upper Division
Writing Courses in Your Major (GWAR)

Your Second-Year Composition Requirement (2YC)

After completing FYC with a grade of C- or higher (or a grade of Credit), you can begin planning when to fulfill your second-year composition requirement (2YC). So that you are practicing writing in a sustained way throughout your education, you are strongly advised to enroll in 2YC before completing 60 semester units. To fulfill 2YC, you may take ENG 214, or if you prefer a course targeted toward multilingual support, CMS 310.

2YC asks students to build on what they have learned in their FYC course in order to advance their writing fluency to the next level. The pace of 2YC is quicker than that of FYC, and the class size is slightly bigger (25 students), so you will be asked to use what you have already learned to self-direct your learning.

2YC asks students to build on what they have learned in their FYC course in order to advance their writing fluency to the next level.

As you can see in the 2YC course description below, 2YC emphasizes developing more flexibility in your reading and writing practices so that you can successfully tackle a wide range of writing situations or tasks. 2YC also asks you to develop more advanced research skills, to practice responding to a wider variety of ideas and perspectives, and to create more sophisticated academic arguments in your writing. The course description for 2YC reads as follows:

> Second year composition is designed to help students develop flexible reading and writing skills as they engage with academic argumentation and inquiry and with real-world issues. Students create varied, rhetorically aware compositions; they reflect on writing practices, processes and strategies; and they incorporate feedback to globally revise drafts. To develop responsible positions, students fine-tune research skills, evaluating scholarly and non-scholarly sources and incorporating a variety of perspectives.

To compare how 2YC builds on and extends what you've learned in FYC, consult the table below, which shows the progression in expectations and outcomes:

FYC Reading and Writing Goals | 2YC Reading and Writing Goals

FYC Reading and Writing Goals	2YC Reading and Writing Goals
Read **actively and effectively** and use information acquired from readings, research and other sources critically in their own writing	Read **analytically and critically, complex texts** representing **varied cultural and academic frameworks**, integrating multiple perspectives
Use **writing processes and strategies** for generating, revising, editing, and proofreading their work; collaborate with others during the writing process, developing ways to offer constructive criticism and accept the criticism of others	Adopt **task-specific strategies** for generating, drafting, editing and proofreading, and revise mindfully, refining ways of giving and using feedback
Reflect on their reading and writing processes as an avenue to achieving greater control of these processes and increased effectiveness as readers and writers	**Reflect on their own and others' literacy processes, strategies and habits** towards **more flexible** reading and writing skills

FYC Rhetorical Knowledge Goals	2YC Rhetorical Knowledge Goals
Demonstrate a **basic familiarity with rhetorical conventions**, composing effective expository prose with regard to purpose, audience, and genre	Compose **rhetorically aware, complex prose** in appropriate genres, matched to purpose, audience, and context

FYC Research Goals	2YC Research Goals
Create and apply **a research plan** to **locate, use, and evaluate information** from a variety of sources, including library resources	Employ **advanced search strategies** to examine, and advanced criteria to evaluate, a wide variety of sources, including library resources, **distinguishing scholarly from non-scholarly and primary from secondary information**
Use **evidence and analysis to successfully support** the central purpose of their writing; demonstrate ethical conduct in their writing and the appropriate use and citation of the works of others	Use evidence from **a variety of sources** to support a purpose, **distinguish adequate from inadequate support**; use and cite information properly and ethically

FYC Genre/Convention Goals	2YC Genre/Convention Goals
Develop knowledge of genre conventions ranging from structure and paragraphing to tone and mechanics; control such surface features as syntax, grammar, punctuation, and spelling	**Control rhetorical and grammatical features**, including style, usage, and conventions, with attention to purpose, audience, and genre

FYC Experience Goals	2YC Experience Goals
Gain and use **knowledge of the academic community** to support their development as learners, readers and writers	Inquire into **authentic social issues** and **enter into scholarly conversations**, articulating **responsible, informed positions**

Your Final Writing Requirement: Upper Division Writing Courses in Your Major (GWAR)

Your upper division writing requirement will be satisfied by a writing-intensive course in your chosen major. Here at SFSU, we call the last class towards your university writing requirement GWAR courses (which stands for Graduation Writing Assessment Requirement). All of the CSUs have some kind of GWAR requirement. Here at SFSU, an intensive writing class in your chosen major allows you to build on what you have learned in FYC and 2YC in order to learn the types of writing used in your chosen discipline. Writing in your GWAR class will not only help you learn specific content in your major, it will also help you practice writing in the genres and styles used by professionals within your chosen discipline.

Writing in your GWAR class will not only help you learn specific content in your major, it will also help you practice writing in the genres and styles used by professionals within your chosen discipline.

Like FYC and 2YC, your GWAR course will usually be small (25 students or less) and will stress revision. Although you will likely find yourself using and adapting many of the reading and writing strategies you have learned in FYC and 2YC, you will also learn more specific practices and conventions that pertain to your major. In this regard, your instructor will be an invaluable guide, since she not only understands what constitutes successful writing within your field, but also has a deep understanding of the content of your field.

In GWAR, your instructor will discuss with you the conventions of writing in your discipline throughout the term, as well as provide feedback on your writing. As in FYC and 2YC, you will be asked to regularly revise your work and perhaps to make use of helpful revision tools like peer review. As you work to develop the more specific types of writing required by your major, your instructor will likely sequence assignments so that you are able to build toward a longer writing project or paper.

In sum, your GWAR class gives you the chance to practice integrating knowledge from your major with your knowledge about writing. In GWAR, you will learn the specific ways of asking questions, reporting information, making arguments, and presenting ideas that your chosen field values. And, because your GWAR course is situated within your major, GWAR thus helps you continue your journey toward being a successful writer, no matter what your future field may be.

■ *When should I take GWAR and how do I enroll?*

After you've completed 2YC with a grade of C- or higher (or a grade of Credit), you may enroll in a GWAR class in your major. Check the course schedule, as well as the Approved Course List (http://wac.sfsu.edu/content/approved-gwar-courses)

to see which GWAR courses are required for your major. Some majors have multiple courses that will fulfill the GWAR requirement. The College of Business, the College of Science and Engineering, and the College of Ethnic Studies offer college-wide courses that will satisfy the requirement for specific majors.

Additionally, some majors have courses that are offered in both GWAR and non-GWAR versions. You'll need to check the course schedule carefully for a "GW" after the course number to make sure that the version of the course you are registering for fulfills GWAR. Since some GWAR classes act as portals to the major and others require prerequisites, consult with your major department and/or your advisor for advice about when you should take your GWAR course. You can also check with your department/advisor about whether your GWAR course will be counted as a requirement toward your major or as an elective (this varies by department).

■ What if I need additional support while in my GWAR class?

In addition to GWAR-oriented resources at the LAC and CARP (see Chapter 6 for more information), students who feel they need more writing practice than GWAR provides should consider taking one of the two courses below:

English 418: Grammar for Writers

ENG 418 is intended for those who would like to improve their writing through the study of grammatical sentence structures.

English 415: Grammar and Editing for Multilingual Students

English 415 is an upper-division grammar and editing course designed to be taken concurrently with GWAR. The course offers instruction and practice in editing for accuracy and style, as well as correct use of citations. Students will also learn to understand and fulfill the requirements of diverse writing tasks.

■ Can I earn credit for taking both a GWAR version and a non-GWAR version of the same course?

Some courses are offered as both a GWAR version and a non-GWAR version. You should know that if you have completed a course section with a GW suffix you may NOT repeat and earn additional units for a non-GWAR section of the same numbered course. The reverse is also true: if you complete the non-GWAR section of a course you cannot take the GWAR version and earn credit. Thus, a student who takes both PLSI 360GW and PLSI 360 would earn just 4 units total. You should check with your advisor if you have further questions about this issue.

■ *What if I don't have access to a GWAR course in my major because of scheduling or other issues?*

All majors have approved GWAR courses at this point; however, adoption of GWAR courses is ongoing so some majors are continuing to design their course offerings. In the extremely rare case that you don't have access to a GWAR course, ENG 414 will satisfy the university requirement. Check with your major department or advisor if you have questions about which classes count towards fulfilling your GWAR requirement or email wac@sfsu.edu.

Completing Your University Writing Requirement

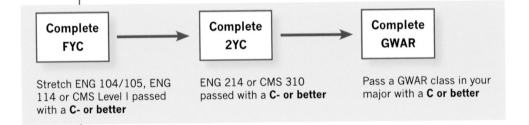

Complete FYC	Complete 2YC	Complete GWAR
Stretch ENG 104/105, ENG 114 or CMS Level I passed with a **C- or better**	ENG 214 or CMS 310 passed with a **C- or better**	Pass a GWAR class in your major with a **C or better**

General Campus Resources

One Stop Student Services Center

Scholarships

Disability Programs and Resource Center (DPRC)

Counseling and Psychological Services Center (C & PSC)

Student Health

Veterans Services

The resources and academic support described in Chapter 6 are designed to offer students support particularly while they are enrolled in FYC courses. Here in Chapter 10, we offer you information about some general campus resources available to you throughout your time at SFSU. We hope you'll take advantage of many of these sources of support.

One Stop Student Services Center

The One Stop Student Services Center, which is located in the lobby of the Student Services Building, is a place where you can take care of a number of important tasks. Here, you can get and add money to your OneCard student identification, register and pay for classes, talk to a financial aid counselor, register for tests, and access your grades and records.

Scholarships

Department of English Language and Literature Scholarships Page	Website: http://english.sfsu.edu/content/scholarships-fellowships-and-financial-aid
College of Liberal and Creative Arts Scholarships Page	Website: http://lca.sfsu.edu/pages/scholarships
Office of Student Financial Aid	Phone: (415) 338-7000 TDD: (415) 338-4321 Email: faschol@sfu.edu Student Services Building One-Stop Center Website: http://www.sfsu.edu/~finaid/scholarships/

The Department of English Language and Literature maintains a webpage about scholarships and fellowships available to students in the department. The page is updated as new offerings become available, so be sure to check back each semester to see whether scholarships for which you might be eligible have been posted. Likewise, the College of Liberal and Creative Arts maintains a scholarship page which is updated as new offerings become available. Other departments also offer scholarships, so be sure to check department websites and bulletin boards for further opportunities.

The Office of Student Financial Aid maintains a scholarship website which compiles information about many current scholarship opportunities, as well as tips on how to find scholarships, how to complete scholarship applications successfully, information on how to deal with scholarship money when it's time to file your taxes, and suggestions on how to avoid scholarship scams. If you have scholarship questions, you can even make appointments to meet with advisors.

If you have scholarship questions, you can even make appointments to meet with advisors.

In addition to scholarship opportunities, you may also want to consider pursuing opportunities to showcase a research project, if you are pursuing an interesting and rigorous research project as an undergraduate. SFSU hosts both an undergraduate and graduate research competition near the beginning of the spring semester, and the California State University system coordinates a system-wide student research competition (hosted at a different CSU campus each year) later in the spring. For more information, visit the Division of Graduate Studies webpage, which has more information about the competition, at http://www.sfsu.edu/~gradstdy/research-competition.htm.

Disability Programs and Resource Center (DPRC)

Phone/TTY: (415) 338-2472	Student Services 110
Email: dprc@sfsu.edu	Website: http://www.sfsu.edu/~dprc/

The Disability Programs and Resource Center can help you work with your instructor to make sure that you get appropriate educational accommodations. Some students are hesitant to seek disability accommodations, especially for milder or "invisible" disabilities, such as ADHD. But it can be hard to know in advance whether or not you'll need an educational accommodation for any given class, so it's a good idea to work with the DPRC even if you don't think you'll end up needing accommodations; that way, if you do realize you need it, the documentation process will already be complete, and all you'll need to do is talk to your instructor.

The Disability Programs and Resource Center can help you work with your instructor to make sure that you get appropriate educational accommodations.

NOTE

Verifying your eligibility for accommodations takes time, and arranging some accommodations can take up to four weeks, so start the process early—before the beginning of the semester, if possible. The process is explained in detail on the DPRC website.

Counseling and Psychological Services Center (C & PSC)

Phone: (415) 338-2208	Student Services 208
TDD: (415) 338-4321	Website: http://www.sfsu.edu/~psyservs/

College can be stressful, and many students find it challenging making the transition from high school to college. In addition, college students may, like the general population, struggle with eating disorders, substance abuse, inter-personal or family conflicts, depression and anxiety, issues relating to sexuality or sexual orientation, and other concerns. The Counseling and Psychological Services Center (C & PSC) is here to help you, should you need it.

Appointments can be made at the C & PSC office in room 208 of the Student services building, or by calling (415) 338-2208. If you experience a crisis outside of normal office hours, the center has compiled an extensive list of off-campus emergency services, which you can find by following the "Emergencies" link on the C & PSC website. Among these are free and confidential national hotlines which you can call if you are in need of help:

- 1-800-SUICIDE or 1-800-784-2433

- 1-800-273-TALK or 1-800-273-8255

- TTY: 1-800-799-4TTY or 1-800-799-4889

Do not hesitate to dial 911 in the event of a medical or psychiatric emergency. When you dial 911 from a campus phone, your call will be routed directly to campus emergency services.

When you dial 911 from a campus phone, your call will be routed directly to campus emergency services.

The counselors and faculty of the C & PSC include psychologists, social workers, and marriage and family therapists, which enables the Center to offer personal counseling and psychotherapy, group counseling, marriage and family therapy, and referral services for students who need services not available on campus. Check out the C & PSC website to find out more about services, including wellness tips and a list of current group topics: recent groups included an anger management group, a meditation group, and a Chicana/Latina support group.

Student Health

Phone: (415) 338-1251   Student Health Center
Website: http://health.sfsu.edu

The Student Health Center may meet many of your health needs while you are a student at SFSU. In addition to serving as the primary healthcare provider for many students, the Student Health Center also promotes health awareness throughout the larger campus community. Visit the center's website for more information on enrolling in a health insurance program, clinic services, the nutrition clinic, women's services, and more.

It's hard to do your best work when you are under the weather, so we recommend that students take advantage of the low-cost immunization clinic. Spread great ideas in your FYC class—not the flu.

Veterans Services

Phone: (415) 338-2336	Student Services 206
Email: veterans@sfsu.edu	Website: http://www.sfsu.edu/~veterans/

The Veterans Services Center provides information and support for student veterans, active duty personnel, reservists, and eligible dependents. The center can help students start or transfer educational benefits, offers advice for students as they go through the process of filing Veterans Administration claim forms for federal and state education assistance programs, and provides assistance with special registration procedures for students sponsored under VA Fee Waiver programs.

Continuing students who are veterans or current active-duty members of the U.S. armed forces are eligible to register for classes on the first day of priority registration. If you are a veteran or current active-duty servicemember, visit the Veterans Services website or contact the center to submit the appropriate documentation so that you can receive this benefit.

A campus student organization, VETS @ SFSU, also provides support for student veterans and their family and friends at State. VETS stands for Veterans Education Transition and Support. The club provides a space for veterans to meet and talk to other veterans, and serves to educate the campus community about veterans. The VETS website can be found at http://sfstate.orgsync.com/org/vets.